Grow your Business with
Online Courses:

How experts and small business owners use their online courses to get more clients, increase revenue per client, make clients come back more often, and decrease marketing expenses

Dimitris Bronowski

Dedication

They say that not the necessity, but the coincidence is full of magic. I always felt strange when discussing coincidences. My bachelor degree was in theoretical physics, so I consider coincidences natural. It would be quite unlikely to live a life without coincidences.

On the other hand, I love studying human psychology. There, I found out that we don't understand the meaning of our experiences; we forge it. And this simple action, makes us see meaningful coincidences.

This book is one of those coincidences. A random selection of links led me to meet Gerdy Heek, a Dutch entrepreneur, living 1400 miles away from my home. Gerdy trusted me and gave me responsibilities beyond my capacities. And I accepted it. Then Gerdy introduced me to Nisandeh Neta, a multimillionaire marketing expert who changed the course of the Dutch economy. And a random decision to eat in a restaurant instead of my hotel room led me to find a way to help him. And then he trusted me, and gave me responsibilities beyond my capacities. And I accepted it. We kept working together, and he trusted me more. And gave me even more responsibilities. Once again, I accepted it.

After big failures and small successes, those two coincidences, those two people, led me to a path of a more meaningful life, where my work has a purpose far greater than me, and my vision defines my daily actions.

Thank you Gerdy. Thank you Nisandeh.

Table of Contents

About the author

Dimitris Bronowski is helping experts and small business owners increase their profits by using online courses and referral/contact/digital marketing.

He has worked as the CEO of the largest business training company in the Netherlands, Open Circles Academy, while it was transitioning to offering its services digitally through online courses. He also managed as CMO the global marketing operations of BodyBrainDance, a company with the vision to help millions around the world fight mental and physical degeneration.

His love for marketing, networking and all things digital, led him to create Networks of Influence. There he helped small business owners grow their businesses by building relations with key individuals, structuring referral marketing systems and using online courses.

He is also the author of the book *Landing your Dream Job: No CVs. No Cover Letters*, which helped individuals all around the world get their dream jobs in companies like Google, Amazon and others, even if that meant transitioning into professional areas they had no previous experience in.

Dimitris has also worked with many small businesses and projects focused on helping people grow their businesses, improve the quality of their lives, reconnect with nature, protect their minds and bodies.

His values are family, growth, calmness and gratefulness. He currently lives with his family in Portugal, close to the ocean, trying his luck surfing its beautiful waves, and helping remotely businesses grow all around the world.

For more information, visit:
growyourbusinesswithonlinecourses.com.

The Goal

This book has a simple goal: To help experts and small business owners like you understand how to use a simple online course that they can create in less than a week, to get more clients, make more revenue per client and make their clients buy more often their services. If you choose this course of action, you won't need any special skills to apply this strategy beyond your ability to talk about your topic of expertise and the ability to use the camera of your mobile.

This strategy or its variations has been tested again and again on an audience of 150000 business owners, by the fastest growing business training company in the Netherlands, Open Circles Academy (OCA). At the time of this writing, I am the CEO of OCA, and I am proud to say that according to a conservative estimation of one of the most prominent newspapers of the country, OCA has brought more than 250 Million Euros to the Dutch economy till now.

Let's start with a simple clarification. When I am using the word "Expert", I am referring to anyone who has developed an in-depth knowledge of her field. You might be a life coach, a business consultant, a nutritionist, a masseuse or massage therapist, a stress expert, or anything else that requires you to have specialized knowledge of what you are doing.

A requirement for this strategy to work is that you are helping people achieve at least one of the following:

- Increase their income
- Save money
- Live a better life

- Save time

If you are doing any of the previous or a combination of them, then the strategy I am going to describe next is something that you can apply immediately. Now, let's take a look at the main problems experts have. Make sure to identify to what extent you are dealing with those problems, so that we can work together on dealing with each one.

First, lately it is getting more expensive to get new clients. Advertisement costs go up, and prospects are getting more and more of what it has come to be called "ad blindness." If you ever knew that there was an advertisement banner at the right of a website without even looking at it, and just scrolled down without checking what it is, then you know exactly what ad blindness is: *your* clients not seeing *your* ads.

Second, a lot of clients come only few times for your service, and then they stop coming back. We call that "the problem of non-returning clients". This forces you to look for new clients instead of just providing your services to your existing ones. You are also reducing one of the most important metrics of your expert business: the average profit per client. This metric is crucial. If you have a high average profit per client your business is going well. Anything that reduces this number is an indicator that your business is underperforming. The good thing is that this is one of the simplest problems you can solve, and we'll see how as we go on.

But the problem of non-returning clients has a second significant effect: your clients do not manage to get the improvement and the results they were looking for when they came to you in the first place. They came to lose a lot of weight, and they went back home disappointed that they didn't manage. They came to increase their self-esteem, and they left feeling the same. They came to learn how to build a better business, and they just started to know about your strategies, but left before implementing them. They came to cure a chronic pain or fix their nutrition and... you get the idea. This is a guaranteed way not to see those clients again. They just remember that you didn't deliver, although we both know that it was them quitting too early.

When clients stop receiving your services before getting results you are not benefiting from, in my opinion, the most important source of clients for experts: referrals. A satisfied client will give referrals, especially if you give her the right incentives. A dissatisfied client will not, even if you provide great incentives.

After being the CEO of OCA and seeing how the right referral system helped build a 23 million dollars expert business, I can tell you with absolute certainty: your clients generating referrals for your business is one of the most sacred elements of your marketing. Experts that don't get at least 50% of their clients due to lack of a referral system are just keeping their business small. Thankfully, once again, this is one easy problem to solve, and we'll see together how you can increase your referrals soon.

The next problem most experts face is that they feel overworked and underpaid. The reason usually is that the average profit per client is low. The simple realization of the origin of the problem might already give you a pick to the solution. If you knew how to increase the profit per client without working more, then you would be able to start feeling that your time is well spent. In the following chapters we'll see how to do that.

The last problem we are going to tackle is something that baffles a lot of experts. Although their service is good, they don't get referrals. We already saw before one of the reasons for that. But even when the service is good, getting referrals might still be hard. To get referrals, you need an exceptional service *and* a referral system. But how do you transform a good service to an exceptional service without having to work a lot more, possibly increasing a lot the costs of operating your business? And then, how do you build a referral system without spending much time or money doing it? We'll answer those questions in the next chapters, where you will see that you will not only increase the number of referrals that are coming from your clients, but that you can also get new clients due to referrals that were generated by the clients of other professionals.

To summarize, the problems that most experts have are the following:

- Not enough clients
- Not enough returning clients
- Not enough revenue per client
- Not enough referrals.

The result is that those experts work more hours, get paid less, and spend more time and energy on marketing their services than actually providing them. Also, they spend more money advertising their services instead of investing this money to improve the services they provide, keeping their business small, instead of making it have a global reach.

By the end of this book, you will have a clear way to get more clients, more returning clients, more profit per client and more time, energy and money to invest in your business instead of spending it to get clients. To do that, you won't need to have any other skill except what you already possess: your ability to talk about the topics you love.

Before we close this chapter, I would like to tell you a bit of why I am writing this book and why I believe there is something in this book that you need to listen to grow your expert business.

I have worked as the Chief Marketing Officer for different expert businesses that saw massive growth. One of them was helping people become happier, healthier, wealthier and wiser, and it grew in one year from 0 to a bit over 400000 Euros. Its name is HappyHealthyWealthyWise (HHWW), and it was the child of a fun project that was called 0toMillion. The idea there was to build and grow a business in one year, and make it generate 1 Million Euros. But there were some conditions: the founder would start with no team, no office, no product, no mailing list, just a tablet, and only 100 Euros. Plus, he would work only two days per week to achieve it. What happened after a few months? Rooms were consistently filled with clients that wanted to learn how to improve their lives in the four areas of happiness, health, wealth and wisdom. Our main expert shared his expert knowledge on stage, reaching hundreds of people at once. As the business grew, I created and managed advertisement campaigns on a $100k Facebook account, created videos and helped build online marketing funnels.

HHWW later gave birth to another company called Life Plan Design. There we helped people design their ideal life, with a unique method that makes you look into your past to find the messages life gives you, *before* looking forward, in order to create your life's plan. During that period we used blogging, combined with email marketing and online marketing funnels and webinars to reach 45000 people. Moreover, we used a method that was developed in Open Circles Academy to write a book in 28 days, and used this book to build the expert position this business needed to attract the right clients.

Following that, I became the CEO of Open Circles Academy (OCA). OCA generated 23 million dollars by helping experts grow their businesses. This was achieved by providing unique courses that helped them understand how to market their business, how to position themselves as experts in the eyes of their clients, and how to use that position to increase their prices, attract the right clients and become financially free on the way, while helping others improve their lives. In OCA, rooms of about 1000 coaches, consultants, solopreneurs, healers, practitioners, and small business owners were filled every few months. And they were all looking for the same thing: a simple process to grow their business and stop feeling overworked and underpaid. If you haven't guessed it yet, the main way to acquire those clients was simply: referrals.

Now, a lot of the live courses OCA offered costed all the way up to $4000 per person. The clients were fully committed to changing their businesses. As the time passed, it was decided to put those courses online, and this way reduce the cost of the courses, so more people can get a chance to learn from them. The courses helped experts reduce their workload, increase their revenue, make getting clients easier and finally, become financially free, meaning that they were now able to stop working should they choose to for any time duration without negatively influencing their lifestyle or earnings.

While working in OCA, I got deep into the essence of all the courses, which combined have an estimated worth of almost 50 thousand Euros, and saw how different expert businesses were built and grew.

And this is why I decided to write this tiny book. To give you the ONE strategy that can give you more clients, more profit per client, more returning clients, more referrals, and more free time for you. And since I know that the most valuable resource you have is time, I made sure to create a solution that will demand no more than a few days of work to prepare (I had experts preparing everything in one weekend.)

Now, I am not saying that this strategy will help you solve all your problems. *All I am saying is that if you stay with me, you will see a simple, easily implementable, logical and tested strategy to grow your expert business.* You will see and understand how and why it works, and it might give you a few more ideas that you didn't think of before. Enough with the intro, let's get into it.

Let your clients return more often

Repeat clients are your best clients. Let me say that again. *Repeat clients are your best clients.* Getting new clients costs (usually) money and time. Getting new clients most of the times demands that you shift your attention from your services to *marketing* your services. Getting repeat clients demands that you focus on your service. Which one do you love doing? As I said, repeat clients are your best clients.

But why some clients leave after receiving your services once or twice, and others stay for years? To make it even more specific and actionable: *why do clients return?*

The first reason a client will return might be that you are the only one offering a specific service. Now, most people think that this is extremely difficult to happen. If you are a life coach or psychologist how can you possibly be the only one providing a specific service? Over the years we have discovered many ways to differentiate your service. It might be as simple as creating your own system, which is a lot easier than you might think. In Open Circles Academy clients built their own systems in less than a day. On the other side of the spectrum, you can simply add a foot massager and a unique variety of tea that you import. Imagine arriving at a waiting room, and you see a simple foot massager waiting for you, in front of the couch. You just need to put your feet on it and click the button. When your session starts after that, you will be already in a good comfortable mood, allowing you to have a great session. How difficult is that? We have discovered hundreds of ways to differentiate services over the years, and we saw that 95% of the times, it is a lot easier than people think. If this is idea seems interesting, you can find out more on the resources page growyourbusinesswithonlinecourses.com/resources.

The second reason clients return is because they started with you something that hasn't been completed yet. Most professionals are well aware of this. At the end of each session with a life coach or a consultant, you will often realize that they will start mentioning another topic that you need to work on. They will not complete the discussion; they will just create an "open loop", something that you need to come back and "close" the next time. If you don't have that in your service, try to include it and see the results for yourself.

A variation of that is what we call "Promise of future value for loyalty". Receiving a free lunch after you went to the same restaurant for ten times is a simple version of it. "Get the third session for free", is a good enough reason to come for a second session. Although these reasons work well, they cost the business owner money and time. Later on, we'll discuss how to apply the same principle without using those resources.

The third reason clients return is because the value they received was way higher than what they feel they paid for. Now, you need to keep in mind that the value a client receives is the sum of the Real Value plus the Perceived Value. A quick tip: the easiest, less expensive and less time-consuming ways to increase the value are:

- Increase the Perceived Value your clients receive or
- Add Real Value that was not generated by you, but from another professional that would like to get known by your clients.

Value a client receives= Real Value + Perceived Value

For example, if you are providing life coaching services, there are plenty of nutritionists out there that would love to give you something of high value for your clients for free. This can help them get new clients. If they are currently spending 50-150$ in ads to get a new client, wouldn't it make sense for them to offer their book for free to you so that you can add it as a bonus to your services? Your clients not only get to receive your coaching, but they leave the session with a free, practical book on nutrition that might improve their lives even more. You over delivered. As long as your nutritionist partner has clearly defined the profile of the clients you should give the book, she will also get high-quality prospects for her business.

If you think that writing a high-quality book takes too much time, think again. We had plenty of clients who wrote their book in less than 28 days. We developed a system for that, that allows you to write without facing "the writer's block" and helps you create a book ready for publishing. Moreover, this book is optimized for marketing purposes so that when your ideal clients read it, they can see that you can help them and by the time they call you, you have already built the necessary trust. Conversions from callers to clients as high as 92% were achieved using this method. Describing the book writing method here would take us away from the purpose of the book, so if you are interested in learning more, check growyourbusinesswithonlinecourses.com/resources. In a while, we'll discuss another great way to use the same principle to get clients, that will cost you a lot less than what you are currently paying to acquire new clients.

The next reason clients come back is because *you made sure they remember of **their** reasons to come back* more often. Think about it: those clients came to you for a reason. They had a great session with you (maybe even received a great tea and a foot massage). They went back home. Life happened. They forgot about their reasons. You are out.

That's how it works. But what would happen if you had a way to help them remember *their* reasons more often?

How do you make people remember of you? Glad you asked. There are two types of reminders: physical reminders and digital reminders. We'll soon discuss the usage of online courses as a digital reminder, but to fully grasp the concept, let's see a couple of examples of physical reminders.

A book is a physical reminder. It is easy to remember someone's services when you see their book on your shelf. And that will help you remember the great session you had and what you got out of it. Now, there are effective physical reminders and ineffective physical reminders. The same object can be either, unless you are aware of the difference. I have worked with many companies helping them create physical reminders of their services. My insight for this book is this: the effectiveness of a physical reminder depends on

- how easily it reminds people their reasons to ask for your services and
- how strongly it indicates where they should place it.

Take a moment to read the previous sentence twice because this might be costing you a lot of money right now. It might be costing you the amount you spent to create the reminder, but even worse, it might be costing you not seeing this client again.

Let's see an example of how not taking into account those two elements might be costing you money. Imagine for a moment that you own a spa, and you currently give a business card to your clients after the service. Is the business card you are giving personalized based on the specific service they came in for? If they came for a massage, does the image on the front of the business card reminds them of the benefits of a massage or they all receive the same business card with your jacuzzi on the front? Remember, you need to remind them of *their* reasons to come back. This simple choice of picture might be costing you clients right now. Creating a few different types of business cards probably costs you less than what you make per client. Print them, and you will recover the cost fast.

Before explaining how to influence where they position their physical reminder, let me say this: What differentiates great businesses from businesses that stay small, is the inability of their founders to understand Return on Investment (ROI). Imagine you are paying now 100$ for your business cards and you get only 20 clients coming back for a second time during a month and paying you 100$ per session. That's 2000$ of income. Now, imagine that you need to decide if you need to pay 400$ to create a different type of cards instead, and those new business cards are 10% more effective. If you take the second decision, in two months you will have covered the cost. After that, you will keep making profits. If you decide to change, by the end of the year you will have avoided losing 2000$ of additional profit.

Most business owners only see the money they invest and the money they receive. *The great business owners see the money they are losing because they are not making the right choices.* Keep that in mind.

Now, let's get back to the second effectiveness requirement: how strongly this business card that you gave indicates *where* it should be placed? Let's follow the path: you give the business card together with a flyer maybe. Your client puts them both in her bag. They probably stay in there for a couple of weeks till she decides to clean and organize the bag. She pulls out your card, the flyer, a couple of other flyers and cards she collected and, you guessed it, throws them in the garbage or best case scenario, arranges the cards together with all the other cards she collected over the years. Your card does not bring a happy memory in her mind; it just forces her to make yet another decision in her life: should I keep it? Where? Should I throw it?

Now, let's see where the "how strongly it indicates where you know they should place it" principle can help us. How can we make her put your business card in a preferred location? This naturally leads us to ask: what is a preferred location? I would love to have my cards somewhere where people see them often. The more often they see them, the more often they remember of me. Wouldn't it be great if she would put your card on the fridge or somewhere that she will see it every morning? Now, a lot of people decide to give magnetic business cards instead of paper business cards. And that is great, as long as your client chooses to put them on the fridge. The truth though, is that most people don't, and your expensive magnetic card ends up in the garbage, probably holding lovingly and tightly a metallic can of her favorite soda.

How do you indicate to your clients to place your magnetic business card on their fridge?

Well, to put it there, they must have a reason to do so, and the reason cannot be simply the fact that they can. I was trying to answer that question, for a long time. One day, while I was reading a book on Contact Marketing (a special type of marketing used to reach VIPs and executives – you can check the resources page growyourbusinesswithonlinecourses.com/resources), I found it. *People will stick on their fridge something that makes them laugh, makes them feel good, makes them feel special.* Now, let's get back to your magnetic business card and use this insight.

Imagine for a second that you are a masseuse and your client, let's call her Meg, decides to organize her bag a couple of weeks after coming to your office. Meg puts her hand inside, pulls out your magnetic card, looks at it, laughs and goes to the fridge. Meg rearranges the other magnets, opening space in the middle. She puts your card right there. What happened? What did Meg saw? Well, it turns out that your card has on it a cartoon, that shows you ready to use some funny looking huge wood massage sticks on a female client (you can't see the face, but the hair give her away) and underneath the caption says: "Meg is always coming here to relax *fully*". If you were Meg, wouldn't you put that on your fridge?

I can tell you with absolute certainty that you would. And I can tell you that, because this simple idea that we so logically ended up to explore, has become a great business for me. I am currently creating personalized magnets for tens of business owners every month. You see, there are some important elements on what a cartoon should or should not do and understanding those elements can be crucial. The wrong kind of cartoon might just have the opposite effect. Some people put their logo or brand name on the caption for example. That kills a cartoon; it makes it feel salesly. Some others forget that only cartoons that reveal truths in a nonintrusive way are powerful. I have come to know instances where clients got offended, since they just got the joke wrong. Finally, a lot of people do not know the right way to personalize the magnet so it can include the name of the client. All those elements allowed me to create a business that offers clients the right type of cartoon, with a caption that makes clients want to stick the business card on the wall.

I am not trying to sell you those offers. I just want to show you how simple logic, combined with marketing insights that I have acquired while managing companies that helped tens of thousands of business owners can lead to unique solutions. In this case, it leads to a simple way to make people remember of you more often.

Now, ask yourself if everything that you give to your clients easily reminds them their reasons to ask for your services and if it strongly indicates where they should place it, so it will keep reminding them of you. You might come up with ideas for improvement, or with radically new ideas.

We used those principles to create some effective campaigns. In one case we targeted executives by giving them a simple, cheap plastic toy with some fluid and a bubble floating inside, together with a message: "what if you could feel like that bubble at the end of each day of work?" Who was our client? A float spa, where you enter in a tub full of salty water that makes you float. We sent those to the offices of potential clients of the spa. Weeks later, they were still on their desk, reminding them of taking care of themselves. Play with those ideas, or simply reach out to me if you want some feedback.

OK, now, we spent a lot of time discussing a small aspect of physical reminders. What about digital reminders? I have to admit; I love digital reminders. And the reason I love them is that once you create them, it costs you nothing to use them again and again exactly at the moments that you believe are the most effective. We have created digital reminders that kept reminding people for years about our services.

There is a second reason I love digital reminders. When you are creating physical reminders, every reminder you give away costs money. So you always try to minimize the cost, or find this one unique solution that has a massive return on investment. But with digital reminders, you have the freedom to invest a bit more to create something unique that will make your clients receive great value, and then, you can use it for free as many times as you want. This allows you to focus on creating something unique. But what are some examples of digital reminders?

Well, if it is not apparent, a digital reminder is anything that digitally reminds people of *their* reasons to come to you. A simple, valuable weekly email can do that. Its effectiveness depends on the understanding the business owner has of copywriting (both for the email itself and its subject line), email automation and compelling calls to action (which simply means making the readers naturally and easily take a specific action such as visiting your website or buying a product.) After having communicated with tens of thousands of people every week over email, I can tell you that it is a beautiful art. It costs nothing to send an email and if you know how to keep your list engaged, you have a money printing machine right there.

There are a few alternatives, such as Facebook bots, SMS services etc, but there is a huge trend now to come back to emails. Why? Because they work.

At the end of the day, any digital tool that allows your clients to remember more often in a meaningful and valuable way their reasons to come to you is a digital tool worth exploring. I experimented with different options over the years. During this time, after working with plenty of companies, there was one method that kept bringing the best results. This method allowed us to:

- deliver more value to clients without spending more money or time,
- remind them of their reasons to come back for more services,
- educate them related to additional reasons to come back,
- offer "future" value for their loyalty
- get easily new clients and
- increase referrals.

If I had to suggest just one thing that you should absolutely do, is the following: create an online course. Creating your own online course requires a lot less time than you might think (you can create a great online course in 3 days) and the only thing you will need to create it is your mobile and a 15$ lavalier microphone. Everything else can easily be taken care by someone else at a minimum cost. Moreover, if you do it the smart way, you will have ideal clients coming to your online courses without you having to pay anything or spending time on promoting it. In fact, other professionals will want to do that for you.

If you decide to use the method I explain below you will be able to get more returning clients, increase revenue per client, and get more clients overall.

In Open Circles Academy we consistently used online courses to bring in clients and generate profit. In fact, in a single promotion a couple of years ago, a few hundred thousand Euros were generated just from our online courses. Now, I don't say that this happened easily. There was a lot of work and understanding of marketing involved. All I am saying is that we have seen it work first hand, and that you can easily replicate part of what OCA did, to increase your business' revenue. And I am going to share with you below how.

First, let me share with you how you can use the online course once it is created. The reason I am doing that, is because I know that if you don't convince yourself of the benefits of having an online course and using it the way I suggest you do, you probably won't create it.

How to use online courses to get more repeat clients

A lot of people think that you can make a lot of money just by selling a course online, in course platforms like Udemy. Although this might be true for some people, it isn't for the majority. To get a respectable amount of income in such platforms, you will need to be in the game for years, be good in online marketing and have invested a lot of money to build your online brand. The golden time for this kind of platforms was between 2010 and 2015. I can tell you that because when we experimented back in 2018 with those platforms I got in contact with plenty of course creators with tens of thousands of students, and they all told me the same thing: we are leaving these big platforms, and we are going to host our courses in our platforms. Now, I chose not to listen to them, and added a few of OCA's low-level courses on Udemy. Using our expertise in digital marketing, plenty of time, the branding and the list we had built over the years, we got a little over 6000 students. That gave us a respectable income, but it involved a lot of hard work that I, later on, found to be unnecessary, since we created a system that is a lot better and easier.

You see, we found out that most people see online courses as a direct way to make money, instead of a way to get more of their existing clients to come back. What that means, is that they see them as an additional business activity, instead of a supporting system. The bad (and good news) is that the real money and business growth is in the later.

Now, let's imagine for a moment that you already created one online course. What would that mean for your business? What are you supposed to do with them?

In our system, when it comes to your existing clients, you can do three things:

- offer it for free,
- offer it as a bonus,
- offer it as a paid option.

Now, to understand how each of those options can help you increase the number of returning clients, you need to know a bit of how our clients and we create online courses. There are three things you will find in each of our courses: value, reminders, information about our services. Let me explain:

The first thing you will find is plenty of value. Since Open Circles Academy's courses are mainly about marketing for small business owners, we make sure that each of the courses contains actionable, valuable information that our students can see, understand and apply immediately in their businesses. Each of those bits of advice, when applied correctly, increases the income of the business owner, giving them a reason to continue watching. We make sure that their time is well spent.

The second thing we do and we advise our clients to do is to gently remind people of reasons to come back to us. Let me remind you the example of the float spa. People are going to a float spa for different reasons. They might want to relax after a hard day of work; they might want a softer skin so they can feel more beautiful; they might want to rest their body and mind so they can live longer, happier lives. We make sure that they are being gently reminded of those reasons during the online course. We have developed many techniques to make sure that those reasons are discussed in a very natural way, so people don't feel that they are being sold anything. The course's purpose is not to sell, but to remind. When people already have reasons to buy from you, reminding them of those reasons is already enough.

The third thing we include in online courses is informing and educating the viewers about our solutions. In the familiar case of the float spa, floating is not the only option. As a client you can have different kind of massages, buy essential oils, or simply purchase unique types of tea that you can't find somewhere else. Once again, we always make sure that this additional information comes as a natural consequence of the story. In the next chapter we'll discuss more about increasing revenue per client.

For the reader that is interested in exploring these topics alone, books like *Made to Stick* and *Pre-suasion* are a good starting point (check the resources page for more: growyourbusinesswithonlinecourses.com/resources). But now, let's see how those three elements work when applied in the three different ways of distributing the course to the clients.

As we discussed, you could offer free access to this course to your existing clients. After you finish a session with them, or after they bought a product from you, you can let them know about the course. We usually suggest offering it as a gift of appreciation for trusting you, or as a reward for some small positive behaviors. We'll cover how to distribute the course later on. The idea is to always make them feel that they won something of value because they made the right choice (trusting you, dieting for a week, investing in themselves, etc). To increase that effect, we usually suggest that you sell this course to people who are not clients for 200-500, but you offer it for free to your clients. This way they are not receiving a "free course", but a valuable resource. *It increases the perceived value of the course.* Let's see the benefits:

Once they start watching the video, they will receive additional value without you having to work more. You are expanding the capability of your business to provide value without the demand of additional time commitment from your side. Then, as they watch the course, *they keep being reminded of their reasons to come to you*. This increases the number of clients that come back, and therefore your income and their results. Now, simply coming back for a second time increases dramatically the probability of coming for a third time, since your clients have "invested" more in your services, taking a bit more ownership of the process. Later on, we'll discuss how we use email and content dripping to help the businesses we are supporting to remind their clients more often about the courses automatically. Finally, when your clients get to be educated by your courses about other services/products you are offering, they might find more reasons to come back.

What we are discussing here is "Education marketing". This is the reason so many people create videos, blogs, and social media posts. They are trying to educate their market for the value of their solutions. The problem is that most of the times, those business owners lack a system of educating while marketing, and can't grab the attention of potential clients long enough to convert them into clients or "repeating clients". The right structure for online courses followed by the right positioning can help you do exactly that. We'll discuss more about it later. Now, let's see the other two options: offer your course as a bonus or as a paid option.

One of the marketing techniques that has generated billions of additional revenue in different businesses is called "stacking". Simply put, stacking is the process of adding additional value to your original offer, so that it becomes progressively more and more attractive for the client. It is based a lot on another marketing tool that is summarized in the sentence: "What you pay attention to, becomes more important." Let's go back to our familiar example. Imagine that you just finished the first flotation session. As you are leaving, you are casually mentally evaluating if you will go back for a second session, which costs 100$. At that moment, the secretary tells you that every client that chooses to do a second session receives free access to a 500$ course on beauty, relaxation, and longevity. Suddenly, if you decide to book a second session, you are paying 100$, and you are receiving 600$ of value. Now this is an offer that seems too good to say no to. The secretary just applied the "stacking" technique.

From a business point of view, once you have the course, you don't need to pay anything extra. You just need to give access to this client by email. But suddenly, you can now increase the value of each service you offer and increase the conversion. Plus, the clients will watch the course and *keep being reminded of their reasons to come to you*. And you don't have to pay for ads to remind them. They *chose* to be reminded.

Finally, you can offer the course as a paid option. Now, we usually suggest to give a huge discount. If the course is worth 500$, you can tell your clients that they can get it for 50$ if they choose to come for a second session. This way, they will pay 150$ dollars instead of 100$, and they will feel that they still have a good deal since they are receiving 600$ worth of services. The reason some business owners decide to add the course as a paid option, is first to increase revenue and second to increase the number of people that will watch the full course. You see, a lot of people might get the course, but not all of them will see it till the end, giving you the chance to remind and educate them about your services many times over. But most people, simply because they paid for it, they will watch it all. There are other ways to increase the number of people that watched the course till the end, and we'll discuss them later on.

The time has come to do some math. Imagine that you are making 80$ per session with a client and that you have 500 sessions per year (that's less than 2 per day). Online courses used as I mentioned above can increase returning clients all the way up to 60%. Let's keep a conservative estimation of 20%. 20% multiplied by 500 sessions gives 100 sessions. These are 100 sessions you wouldn't have otherwise. One hundred sessions multiplied by 80$ is 8000$ bonus. Just by adding a simple course and a conservative estimation you increased by 8000$ the revenue of the business. And we haven't yet considered the effect you can get on increasing revenue per client and the effect on increasing the number of new clients. We will deal with those in the next chapters.

Increase revenue per client

Online courses are a great tool to increase the number of returning clients, and they can be an even better tool to increase the revenue per client. Let's see why.

An online course is something that you create once, and then you can use it repeatedly to generate income without having to work more. This is what we call passive business income. There are six ways to create passive business income sources for you. The online courses belong to one of those six categories, called Digital Resources. The more passive income sources you have, the more revenue you can generate while working less. Once you have built enough passive income sources and the marketing system to distribute them, you can be in an exotic island sipping margaritas. And although this is enticing enough for some people, there is something more deep that happens here: online courses are one of the simplest ways to provide lots of value without having to spend your time. You are basically multiplying yourself. And people are willing to pay for that extra value.

A simple way to do that, is by adding a subscription option to your clients. Below you will see different ways that you can use to do that, so you can choose what fits your business best.

Instead of giving them access to all the videos you have created at once, you release them periodically, one video every week. This way, people will get to receive one value-packed video every week related to topics they are interested in. If you start to think that this might be too much work, stay with me, and you will find a few simple ways to avoid that. And for that service, you can simply charge a 10-20 monthly fee to your existing services.

To see how that would work, imagine that you help people lose weight. You already have your weekly or bi-weekly sessions. But losing weight is not only about what you eat and how (often) you exercise. It is also about motivation, psychology, having someone to inspire you when you are about to make the wrong choice. Well, what if you add videos focused on those areas and release them once every week to help your clients go through the journey? You only need to record 12 short videos, and you have enough content for three months.

If you charge 80$ per session, a lot of clients won't have a problem to add 10-20 per month on that, to have the additional support you offer through your videos. If you have 500 clients per year and even if only 10% of them choose the monthly option, you suddenly make 6000-12000 of additional income (without calculating the extra income due to the increase of returning clients that we mentioned in the previous chapter.) Is it worth it? I say it is.

Now that you slowly see the math, you might have already started realizing that creating more than one course might make sense. Why not have a low-level 10-20 monthly subscription model, and a second model with a more advanced course plus an online live team Q&A session once per week? This way, the clients that are really committed to creating a change in their life and business will have a way to receive additional support, and you can increase the number of times you interact with them and help them with their journey. A lot of clients prefer this "handholding" type of service. This is a great option for a lot of business owners, since it allows you to communicate during the Q&A sessions with a lot of clients at once, saving you time.

Let's see the math here. Usually, this kind of service is offered for 27-47 per month. If you are wondering why these prices, let me tell you that prices ending in 7 seem to convert better. If you do a quick research on online products sold today, you will see it appearing again and again. Obviously, less people will be willing to buy than the ones that bought the first option, and keeping the previous example in mind, let's assume that only 25 people (5% of your clients) will do that (although I have seen way bigger numbers in businesses I have worked with). This translates to an additional 8100-14100 per year. Think about it! Even if you don't have 500 clients per year, and you only have 100 clients, you are still able to create a huge additional income that wasn't there before. Now, if you have even less clients than that, don't worry. In the next chapter I will show you how you can get additional clients using the courses you created. Let's go one step at a time.

Another way to increase revenue per client is to package your services so that they include the online course(s). This is a powerful way to add value to your offering without having to work more for that value. Let's see an example. Imagine that you are helping people build their self-confidence. When they call you to schedule a session you just need to tell them: "Look, I want my clients to create huge results in their lives. To do that, I want to be able to be there for you more often. Since I cannot do that physically, I created a set of videos that can help you get more results in the time between the sessions. Most of my clients find it extremely helpful to have some additional guidance when the excitement of the last session starts to fade away as the days pass. Some others just need to be reminded of what we discussed. For that reason, I created this online resource, so that you can get that support. It only costs an additional 10% of the session's cost to have the complete package. Would you like to have this additional support?" Would you be willing to pay just 10% more to get the complete package? I would.

This way, you just increased your revenue by 10%, while making sure that your clients remember of you more often and get educated about your other services. If you think about it, *your clients just paid you to market your services to them.* Compare that with your current expenses on marketing. How much do you spend per month on your marketing? Now you have a way to offset that cost. And if you are thinking right now "Yeah, but I use my marketing to get new clients" let me say this: You just increased your revenue by 10%. To increase your revenue by that amount you would have to get 10% more first time clients AND you would have to pay to get them. Now, they pay you to market your services to them.

But even if that is not convincing enough, let me tell you that in the next chapter we'll discuss how to use the courses to get more clients. To give you a sneak peek: ask yourself, what is going to happen, if you are part of a team of professionals that serve the same type of clients by offering different solutions? If you are offering massages, this team might consist of a nutritionist, a life coach, an image expert and a longevity expert. What if each one of them had one course to offer, and you could offer all those courses to your clients? They would be able to get a full package of valuable online courses by experts they would have to pay a lot otherwise to learn from. And you are providing them privileged access to that at an extremely low price, just because they are *your* clients. Also, what would happen if the clients of the other professionals could see your courses? You would get a lot more new clients, without paying anything to get them. It is as easy as that. More on that in the next chapter.

Get more clients

We have seen how an online course used the right way, can create more returning clients and can increase the revenue per client. The time has come to discuss how you can use your course(s) to get more clients.

Before we get there, I would love to explain why this is important. Think of it as a quick rule of thumb. If these online courses increased by 10% the revenue per client, made 10% of the clients come back, and brought 10% new clients and

1) Your current annual revenue is 50000$, you will now make 66500$, 16500$ more.

2) Your current annual revenue is 75000$, you will now make 99825$, 24825$ more.

For any other annual income, you simply need to multiply your current income by 1.331.

We have seen professionals increasing more than 20% each of those numbers resulting in 86400$ and 129600$. To find the effect in your business you simply need to multiply your current income by 1.728. Now, this is 36400$ and 54600$ of additional revenue, by simply creating and offering an online course the right way. In a while, I will explain how those higher numbers were achieved, but for now, I just want you to see what you are missing out if you don't join the game. How would your life change if you had an additional 20000$? Would you be able to spend more time with your family? Travel more? Pay your debt faster? Sleep calmer at night? Buy this car you always wanted or go to this spiritual retreat for a month to discover yourself?

Currently, if you wanted to increase your revenue by those amounts, you would have to pay a lot of money for marketing and you would have to work a lot more hours.

Here, you have a way to increase your revenue at a minimum money and time commitment.

If you had to take a decision right now, how much money and how many more hours would you be willing to invest to get the additional revenue that corresponds to your current level of income? Take a moment to write that down. We will use this number in a while. Just make sure you write it in a clear form as this example "I am willing to spend 3000$ and 12 more days of work per year". Now, to increase your revenue by 20000$ you might be willing to spend more than 3000$ or less, and you might be willing to work more than 12 days or less. Just define what would be a good tradeoff for you. In a while, you will be able to use this sentence to decide if the time has come to move forward with this idea.

Now, let's see why online courses can transform potential clients into clients and how you can get your courses in front of new prospects.

The reason online courses are such a great way to transform leads into clients is because of something that is called "Education marketing". In the past, to sell, people used to have a "hard push" approach. Salespeople would brag to their friends explaining how they got the sale by "not taking no for an answer" and by hammering people with the benefits of their goods. However, these times are long gone. People get incredibly resistant the moment they feel you are trying to push them to buy. Education marketing is the alternative. Instead of trying to convince people to buy your service, you educate the people who already look for what you have so that they can understand the benefits of working with you.

When the people who want and need what your service can do for them learn about how your service is doing it, they have no reason not to buy as long as they can afford it. Take a moment to reread the previous sentence. This is the core of education marketing. Now, there are three main ways to get your courses in front of the right people. There are more ways, but those three can already help you see the power of having an online course that is optimized for marketing purposes.

The first way is called "The team courses approach". This amazing system is based on the principle of a "remarkable product". You know you have a remarkable product when the people who decided not to buy it feel they did the wrong choice and lost an opportunity, and the people who bought it started talking about it to other potential buyers. In Open Circles Academy we have a full course on how to create a remarkable product or service, since it is crucial for any business owner that wants to grow his business. One way to create a remarkable product, is by making sure the value a client receives is way bigger than the value he paid for.

A simple way to achieve that is by selling for the same price or giving for free not just one, but 4 to 6 online courses that include a full transition to where your client is trying to go. Before you say "6 courses, are you crazy, you think I have all the time in the world to create courses?" let me tell you that you will only need to create one. Stay with me. The most important part of the sentence is not the "4 to 6 courses"; it is the "where your client is trying to go". Think about it. When a client comes to a dietician he doesn't want to just lose weight. Maybe that's what he says he wants, but we know that what he probably wants at the end of the day is to be able to live a healthy life where he enjoys each part of it with self-confidence, energy, and happiness. He wants to live longer and "die young as late as possible." Having a thinner body is essential, so he can run, move, play and be healthier.

But can you imagine how this person's life would change if he could also get

- a happiness coach to teach him how to create a happier mind,

- a meditation coach to show him how to calm his thoughts,
- a confidence expert to help him have trust in his abilities,
- a relationships expert to help him creating empowering relationships, and
- a vision specialist to help him identify what is the ultimate vision of his life?

Plenty of dieticians attended OCA's courses, and if you ask them, they will tell you that the people who lost most weight were the people who, during the process, where happier, had confidence in themselves that they can do it, had a calm, supportive mind and a clear vision of why they are making this effort. However, you don't need to listen to me. Just imagine a person being in the state I just mentioned and ask yourself: If I was that person and I wanted to lose weight, would I have more chances of achieving my goal if I was happier, confident that I can make it, calm and with a big, meaningful why? If your answer was no, you have no reason to continue reading this book. Please close it, and give it to someone that would agree with the previous statement.

Still here? Great!

When you create all the conditions your clients need to succeed in their goals, you are offering them a remarkable product or service. Getting back to the previous example, the vast majority of your clients will lose the weight they wanted to lose easier. When you start becoming known as "the dietician that brings results" you will have more clients knocking at your door than you can imagine. You will be able to raise your prices, and people will still be willing to pay. You will have to start hiring more people to take care of the clients you don't have time to take care of. You will be invited to speak in front of audiences that would love to listen to your advice. This is the power of a remarkable product.

But how can you create that environment of success for your clients? Simple. Find 3 to 5 other professionals that can create the conditions of success for your clients, and ask them to record a quick course about their topic of expertise. Simply explaining what you learned while reading this book, or sending them a copy, will be enough in most cases to convince them. For now, let's focus on why *you* would want to do it and then why *they* would want to do it.

Your goal is to create an environment of success for your clients and offer a remarkable service. The remarkable service consists of your course accompanied with 3 to 5 other courses from experts that will help your client create the environment of success he needs. You will offer the complete package to your clients, but they will get it either for free just because they are your clients or for the discounted price of only one course (let's say 10$). Now see it from the eyes of a client that comes for the first time to try your services. He wants to lose weight, and after one session with you he did not just start the process of achieving that, but suddenly, without expecting it, he got also a full package of content that will help him build a happier life, one that he always wanted but was never quite sure how to get.

Imagine that at the end of the session with him, you tell him something like "Mr. X, I have been long enough in that business to know that the people who truly succeed in losing weight and staying off from gaining it again, have managed to create a particular environment for themselves. First, they spend a bit of time at home to get deeper into the topics we discuss during our session. Also, they create some habits that make them happier during the process, they have a calm mind that allows them to take the right decisions and sleep deeper, and they have cultivated meaningful relationships. To help you achieve your goal, we have partnered with 4 top experts of the industry in those areas, and we asked them to allow us to give to our clients some of their strategies in the form of a one-hour online course. Now, each of the experts we partnered with sells his/her course for 200$ to his/her clients. We do the same for all the people who are not clients. This means that the total courses package is worth 1000$. However, as part of the partnership, we demanded to allow us to offer the complete package for only 17$ to our clients. We want to create the perfect environment for you to lose the weight you came here to lose and we think that this is a great way to do it. To get it you just need to inform the secretary and provide your email."

This is a compelling offer. Your clients got a 98% discount and a powerful package that will increase their results. Also, you got paid to give them access to your course, which will continue reminding them of the reasons they came to you. However, there is one important benefit we left out.

Each of the other experts whose courses you added to the package, will follow the same process. That means that each one of them will give to their clients the courses package, which includes your course. This way, all the clients of your partners will see your course as well. And you won't have to pay anything for that. Your course will do the marketing for you, and some of those clients will contact you to schedule a session. Each time one of those professionals sells or offers for free the course package, you all benefit.

Moreover, the person who is a client of your partners already trusts them. This means that when they see your course, part of this trust is transferred to you. Starting a professional relationship from a higher level of trust is a proven way to increase conversions and get more clients.

Now, there are a few difficulties that you might face while applying this strategy. I am going to describe them first so that you are aware of them should you decide to implement the "team courses strategy" alone, and then I will offer you a solution and explain how we could take care of all this so that you can focus on your clients. Readers of this book have followed both paths, and you are free to choose the one you feel more comfortable with.

The first difficulty is identifying the right professionals for your team. Choosing who should be part of the team and who shouldn't is crucial. Over the years I have repeatedly seen cases where the fit just wasn't right. Remember: your goal is to build the perfect environment for a person to thrive and go even further than where she thought she wanted to go. In the case of the dietician, you want to help your clients create a happy and healthy life, not just a thin body.

Another example is the approach of Open Circles Academy. The business owners that came to grow their business soon found out that this is not where OCA was aiming to take them. That was only the first stop. First, they learned how to increase their income by 10%. Then they learned how to double their income and double their free time. Then they discovered how to become financially free by generating passive business income. And then, they saw that the ultimate goal is to become what is called an "enlightened millionaire", a millionaire that has as the goal of her life to help others. Many students of OCA became millionaires (one even became a billionaire). However, they all came just to increase their income. So, define where you want to take them, what is the biggest picture, and use that to select the type of partners you need.

The second difficulty is explaining to the partners how to create the script for their videos so they can provide as much value as possible and how to record those videos and with which equipment (especially if they never did something similar before). Furthermore, if they don't have a clear understanding of how to infuse marketing in their courses, then their conversion rates will become lower. There is an additional cost for video editing which can reach relatively easily 500$ to 1000$ or more, plus the time you will need to explain to the video editors how those videos must be edited, and how to optimize them to strengthen your marketing.

Then, comes the part of the online management of the course. Hosting the videos in the right platform and covering the cost for the hosting, managing email communication and technical support related emails. If you plan (and we believe you should) to send a few follow up automated emails to the people who bought the courses in order to make sure you remind them of you more often, then you will also need to know a bit of email automation, and how to increase the open rates of your emails, how to increase the number of people that click on your links etc. Sending emails that are not being opened is just a waste of time, and you don't want that for your business. I am sure you have plenty of emails in your inbox that you plan never to read, so you know what I am talking about.

All these are things you need to keep in mind if you decide to start this journey alone. However, there is another option should you choose to trust our expertise in the topic. We'll take care of finding the right people (unless you have someone already in mind), manage online communication and technical support, show you the exact process you need to create a course in one week, show you the exact equipment you need to have beyond a good smartphone with a camera (the total cost of equipment will be around 40$). Moreover, we'll show you how to optimize the course for marketing purposes, so it converts more clients into repeating clients, we'll edit the videos and host them in an online platform. We'll show you different ways to offer your course to your clients, and more ways to use it to get new clients. If your courses are suitable, we can add them to more teams so that you increase your reach, and more potential clients see your services. In a sentence, we are willing to allow you to focus on simply creating and recording a powerful online course that will increase the number of repeat clients, increase the revenue per client and increase the number of new clients, and we'll show you the method our clients used to create those courses in 7 days or less if you choose to do so.

We have seen the power of this method, so we offer this service for a minimum initial fee plus a small monthly fee for the hosting, online communication, technical support etc. I asked you already before to define how much you would pay to create the course(s) and how many days of work you would be willing to put into it. Go back and check it. In 99% of the cases we ask a lot less than that, so if you are curious to know, just check the resources page growyourbusinesswithonlinecourses.com/resources.

Now, I need to be clear: we don't accept each professional that asks for our services. To make sure that we create powerful teams and combinations of professionals, we have to make sure that the fit is right. We need to know the mentality of each professional, his/her qualifications, experience and vision. We also need to know that our clients are committed to create those courses and offer them to the clients. We love to work with people that can see the benefits of this approach and that are willing to grow and learn with us. Finally, we want to make sure that we all enjoy the process of creation of the courses and that our clients trust our expertise.

Should you decide that our offer is what you need, you can contact us directly using the contact information in our support page. We'll send you a quick 5 minutes questionnaire to understand what your business is about and then we'll schedule a call to understand what you are trying to achieve. During this call, you will be able to understand better the support we provide and discuss the different options.

Now, if we find out that the fit is not right, that doesn't mean you can't create a course either way. Later on, I will share a few essential tips that you need to keep in mind when you create the courses.

Let's move to a couple of other ways we suggest that you use should you choose to create an online course to get new clients. This approach is a combination of contact marketing with online services. I briefly mentioned contact marketing before. It is a specific kind of marketing developed for professionals that want to reach VIP clients (executives, famous people, high net worth individuals). We will not go deep, but you will find a simple idea to reach new clients in a creative way that differentiates you from the competition.

The principle is simple: you identify two objects that communicate the benefits you provide to your potential clients, and send them to the top 20-50 clients you would like to have. You connect each object to a call to action and an offer, in the words of the Godfather, they can't refuse.

Let's break it down showing some examples.

Stu Heinecke decided that he wanted to reach some top executives. Luckily for him, he was a cartoonist. He created a list of the top 20 Fortune 500 CEOs that he wanted to work with. He created one personalized cartoon for each of those businesses, showing a problem they were struggling with. The face of each executive appeared in the cartoon. He revealed the problem in a fun way, so that when the executives saw the cartoon, they simply laughed, acknowledged the truth behind the joke, and invited him to the office. Now, he didn't send the cartoon by email. He decided to print it on thick foam, about 18"×24", and have it physically delivered to the office of the executives.

If you know anything about corporate secretaries of high-level executives, you will know that managing to get your email to the computer of the CEO is just a herculean task. Less than 1% of the emails make it. Do you want to guess how many of the cartoons managed to make it to the offices? 100%. However, that was not all. Many of those executives when they saw the cartoons started taking selfies with them and uploaded them online. Some of them still had the cartoons one year later in a prominent position in their office, and talked to others about them and the guy who sent them. This generated additional clients for Stu. A few months later, Stu built a 20 Million dollar company based on these clients. The cost of his campaign? 100$. That's the power of contact marketing.

A simple object that grabs attention delivered to the right top 20 ideal clients. If you are a life coach, what would it mean for your business to coach the head of a newspaper? Or the HR director of a multinational company? How many more clients would come to you after that? Although there is a beautiful process behind identifying the top 20 ideal clients that can revolutionize your business, I will not get into it. Feel free to reach out if you want to know more. What I want you to keep in mind is this. The essence of contact marketing is

1. Identifying the top 20-50 ideal clients
2. Defining two –cheap- objects that communicate clearly something related to your business
3. Getting the objects in front of the right clients
4. Giving them a call to action they would gladly accept.

If you remember, I mentioned an example of a client that sent a plastic toy with some fluid and a bubble floating inside, together with a message: what if you could feel like the bubble at the end of each day at work? The business was a float spa. Now, if you are an executive and suddenly something like that arrives at your office, you will get curious.

People don't do that anymore. People just send emails or pay for ads right?

What's the next step? The call to action. OK, you got their attention, but you don't want this whole effort to look like a stunt right?

Here is where the remarkable service comes into play. Remember: those top clients can revolutionize your business. The credibility, publicity or reach you can get by merely providing your services to them can make hundreds of other clients come to you. So you need to offer them something they would love. In the float spa example, my client was instructed to provide a free float session, followed by a massage and free access to a 1000$ worth of courses focused on beauty, relaxation, and longevity. Now that's a remarkable offer don't you think?

By now you might be wondering, who was the target? Using our Top 20 Process, we identified that the ideal client profile was women, HR directors of big pharmaceutical companies, aged between 35-55. The additional benefit of that selection, if not evident, is that a single satisfied HR director is all this business needed to get their promotions to the employees of the company. Each employee of that company had now free access to a $1000 package of online courses, and a discount to visit the spa. Happier, healthier and calmer employees are an asset for each company since those qualities increase productivity, and thus business results. Moreover, it reduces internal fights and tension, making the lives of HR directors easier. Was that an offer the directors couldn't refuse? I say it was.

The overall cost of this campaign (excluding consulting costs with our team)? 350$.

Did you see how easily the online course was used as a tool to get the message in front of thousands of employees? The only thing we needed to do was to add a few thousand emails to our course management platform, and suddenly all those people started learning more about the offerings of the float spa. How much would you pay to get a few thousand people to learn about your services? This is the power of online courses when used correctly.

The third way to use online courses to get new clients comes as an application of referral marketing. It is our core belief that each business that doesn't get at least 50% of its clients through a structured referral marketing system is throwing money away. In Open Circles Academy, a simple referral system brought on average more than 90% of the new clients. Every few months a room with about 1000 business owners was filled for a full weekend. About 900 of them came because a friend, partner or acquaintance told them they should come to the Business Bootcamp to learn how to grow their business. Now, the Business Bootcamp generated about 23 million dollars, which means that 90% of it is 20.7 million dollars. 20.7 million dollars that were generated because of referrals. We will not get deep into referral marketing since this is not the focus of this book, but we will discuss how to apply its principles using online courses.

The beauty of an online course is that once you create it, it costs you nothing to add a new person to watch it. It provides value to your (potential) clients, but you don't need to work more for it or spend money & time. You merely need to give them access. What this means is that you can offer it to anyone you want, at will. This is what we are going to use now.

Before we start, I want you to know the core of referral marketing:

Every moment where value is given to a client or value is recognized by a client, is a moment where you can generate referrals. Read this sentence again. Let it sink. Every moment where value is given to a client or value is recognized by a client, is a moment where you can generate referrals. What does this mean?

Let's take a moment where value is recognized. Imagine you just finished a session with a client, and the client says: "Thank you. That was a great session." Till now you probably smiled and responded politely: "You are welcome. This is great to hear." Now, you just found out that the core of referral generation is using moments were value recognized. That's it! That's your moment. Let's change your answer simply to "You are welcome. It is great to hear that. You know it is my vision to help as many people as possible enjoy the benefits you just received. And since you see the value my services bring I would like to ask for your help. I decided to offer my 200$ course for free to people that my clients think can benefit from it. Do you have in mind someone that would appreciate this gift? Do you mind taking a moment to write a few names down?"

What did you just do? You took a moment of appreciation and used it as an opportunity to offer free value to the network of your clients. You gave to your client a way to help their network and thus increasing his status. You gave them a way to express their gratitude. Moreover, you got to help more people with your knowledge and online advice, while getting a few extra potential clients.

The next thing you can do is to create a simple VIP package offer. When one of your clients finishes a great session with you and expresses appreciation, you can simply give them five business cards where you wrote their name on with a pen and tell them: "I am happy you enjoyed this session. You know I am trying to provide as much value as possible to my clients. However, sometimes I have to spend more time marketing my services than actually providing them and improving them for the benefit of my clients. For that reason, I decided to create a VIP package for the friends of my clients. If any of your friends comes in the next month for a session with me, just by showing me this card, they will get a 50% discount on the first session and full access to a 1000$ package of material that will help them live a happier/healthier/wiser/wealthier/(you choose) life."

Again, you took advantage of a moment where value was recognized and used the online courses to create a unique offer.

There are more ways to use the online courses to get more clients and are limited only to your imagination and understanding of marketing of your team or partners. In the previous example, you can skip the 50% discount and the session, and simply offer free access to the 1000$ worth of courses. Again, you are getting your courses to the hands of your potential clients, people that gained access to them because their friends recommended you. Another way is just to ask your clients to share a post on social media about their experience and add a link with free access to your course for their network. People love to share opportunities, and a recommendation from a friend is a powerful tool to get new clients.

Now, to get the full advantage of a referral marketing system, we advise our clients to explore the customer journey and identify each moment that value is given or value is recognized and use it as an opportunity to create referrals. Then, we work together to create more moments where value is given or incentives for clients to express appreciation, and of course, use them to generate more referrals.

I will just give a simple example of how that is done, in case it can spark some ideas. In some consulting and coaching businesses, we saw that clients tend to wait 3-10 minutes in the waiting room. We simply added a foot massager, a 50-90 device. This helped the clients relax and enjoy the moment. The quality of the sessions improved. Once the session was over, and the client was leaving the room, we instructed the business owner to simply ask: "Did you enjoy it?" This repeatedly made clients to express appreciation for it and then, as you probably guessed it, the business owner stated "We are trying to offer the best service to our clients. Recently, we decided to start growing the business, and I would love to show you how you could help us, should you choose to do so." From there on, the business owner offered access to the courses/VIP packages etc. Simple, easy, effective. The cost? 50$ for a foot massager. Why? Because we took the time to identify how value can be added and how to create a simple moment where value is appreciated. To check the foot massager, simply check the resources page growyourbusinesswithonlinecourses.com/resources.

Identifying the customer experience from the first moment that they saw or heard anything about your company till a few weeks after they left your office for the last time is a great tool to understand how to increase referrals. Following that with adding a few more reasons for clients to express appreciation and designing the dialogue that should take place after that, will multiply those referrals. Finally being able to offer something of value that doesn't cost you anything after you created it, is the final touch that can make your full referral system work.

Now, the time has come to discuss one more way of using the courses to get clients. This one will be especially valuable for anyone who feels uncomfortable selling his/her services while networking during events. To start, let me say that I believe most small business owners, consultants, and coaches answer wrong this simple question: so, what is your business about?

This question often occurs during events from potential clients, and most people think they have the right answer, but they don't. OK, that's a big claim, so let me explain and let you decide for yourself.

Let's start with a guess: when you created your elevator pitch for potential clients you put some deep thought into answering the following questions:

- Which is the message I want to communicate?
- How do I show best what I do?
- How do I express in a simple and understandable way the value I provide to the client?
- What differentiates me from other similar professionals or businesses?

If you did that, and if you put extra thought into making the sentence you are now using small and memorable, I might have bad news for you. I believe that you have probably found great answers, but you have been asking the wrong questions.

The most powerful way to create your elevator pitch is to answer the following question first: "What reaction do I want to get?" Over the years, we have experimented with different favorable reactions, but there is one that kept over delivering. It managed to both grab attention and convert prospects into clients.

Let's explore it together. Imagine that you are in an event and a potential client asks you: so, what do you do? The person who asked that question might or might not be interested in what you do. He might or might not care about what you are going to say. He might make casual, polite conversation. If you respond with your usual elevator pitch, the discussion will most probably remain superficial.

What you want is to get him curious, get him to ask you for more information. *The reaction you want to get is a combination of surprise (Aha!) and curiosity (Huh?).* And this can be done if you manage to create an intriguing knowledge gap followed by a pause. I will explain below, but let me give some definitions first:

A knowledge gap is any gap between what the prospect hears and how you are achieving that with your work.

What makes a knowledge gap intriguing? When what you do is extremely relevant to the prospect.

Why a pause? Because of the reaction you want the person to have after you pause.

Now, read the following phrase again: *you want to create an intriguing knowledge gap and then pause.* I will give one example for you to understand how to use it in practice.

When I go to events and I meet experts/small business owners/consultants/coaches (the market for which I have developed my services), and they ask me what I do, I say "I help experts/small business owners/ consultants/ coaches get new clients almost automatically." My goal is to "sparkle" interest. When the person who hears that response is part of my target audience, 95% of the time I get the exact same reaction; a smile, a pause and a question: That's interesting, how do you do that?

This is the response you want from a prospect. *You want the prospect to ask you for more, to be curious, to give you his/her full attention.* When you have achieved to make your potential client ask you for more information, then you have gotten his/her interest and permission to explain more, and you have moved away from a superficial conversation.

One day I was delivering a course on how to get more clients through referrals for your business, when one of the participants who was an accountant said "Yeah, but this applies to professionals that do something interesting or life-changing. How can I do it?". We ended up working with this accountant to refine his message. Now, when people ask him what he does, he answers "I help clients become financially free." I don't need to explain why that works. Small business owners immediately ask him, "Wow, how do you do that?". This lets him explain the different service packages he has developed that help people make more profit in their business while cutting losses.

For now, I want you to keep in mind that the response you want people to have after you give your catchphrase is "Interesting, how do you do that?" This gives you both the stage to explain and the full attention of the prospect. Now, you can explain in more detail. The process of identifying the catchphrase is both science and art, and if you want to create your own alone, I would suggest reading a couple of books on advertisement copywriting and on creating memorable and packed with information sentences (growyourbusinesswithonlinecourses.com/resources).

Now, when I first explain this to the clients, they usually get excited due to the capability of this one sentence to get them the attention of their potential clients. To this, I usually respond: "Actually that's not what this technique is about. *The real power of this technique is that it lets you get permission from those prospects to market your services and stay in contact.*"

Let's see how that works. Most people, when they get asked to explain more, they will carefully start communicating their extended pitch. Although you already have permission to do that and it will indeed bring you some clients, we have seen that this is not the best way. *You see, the prospects that are easier to convert are the ones that have qualified themselves.* Please, take a moment to read that again. *The application of this realization can double your clients.* The prospects that are easier to convert are the ones that have qualified *themselves.* In case you are not familiar with the marketing terminology, a prospect is an organization or potential client who resembles the seller's ideal customer profile but has not yet expressed interest in their products or services. *A qualified prospect is an organization or potential client which has expressed interest in the products or services of the seller.* You want the potential client to express interest in your services *before* you explain those services to them.

In Open Circles Academy, products were often sold from the stage. In one specific occasion, more than a million Euros worth of products were sold. As you can understand, each part of the selling process was carefully planned. Making sure that the audience was qualifying itself was crucial. Questionnaires were handed that would make the audience understand and remember their needs and pain points. Questions were asked to which the audience had to verbally agree if they were the kind of people that could benefit from the services that were about to be offered. The more times the audience qualified itself, the more prospects transformed into clients. *You should never try to sell before your prospects qualify themselves.* This simple technique brought thousands of clients to Open Circles Academy, and you can use it too.

So, how do you make your prospects qualify themselves? The moment they say "Interesting, how do you do that?", instead of following the tendency to pitch, simply say "I will explain, but to make sure we are using our time productively, is this something that can somehow benefit your business? What do you do?" This way, first you show that you are not like other people. You are not just looking for an opportunity to pitch and talk about you and your business. You are interested in other people and using your and their time productively. You don't look needy and always looking for other clients. You are in control of the conversation. You are not planning to spend your time explaining something without making sure it is valuable to the other person. You are giving your prospect a stage to talk about himself or his business. Everybody likes to talk about the things that matter to them and be the center of attention. You are setting a favorable environment.

However, this is not the only thing you achieve with that question. You don't want just to pitch. You want to pitch in the most relevant way for the prospect. Moreover, you want to know precisely why he/she should enter your marketing funnel (I will explain that in a while).

Once the prospect explains what their business is about, your job is to listen carefully and in some cases ask questions that will make the prospect mention problems that your services can solve. This will give you everything you need to pitch correctly, or it might just show you that this person doesn't have a problem that you can solve. If the second is true, just say: "Well, it seems that this is not something I can help you with. You see, I only focus on people that are struggling with X, Y, and Z." Remember, you are not trying to sell to everyone. You are trying to sell to people that need your services. However, simply stating X, Y and Z either way, you make sure that if someone else that is listening to this conversation is a potential ideal client, then you will grab his/her attention. If that happens, you simply need to ask them why this is interesting for them.

OK, let's see what happens when a prospect has qualified himself. Time to pitch right? Well... maybe. If the fit is obviously great, and the prospect seems ready to buy, and you are great in pitching, then yes, you can pitch. But, if you feel there is still a bit of work that needs to be done, that the prospect has doubts or is not clear on his descriptions, I would suggest doing something different. This is the time to say: "Interesting! Well, it seems that what I do might be what you are looking for, since I help professionals/people like you achieve X, Y, and Z. But before offering my services, I like to make sure that they are exactly what you need at this stage of your business/life. I have created a course that helps people solve <here you add one or more of the main pain points that the prospect mentioned>. I sell it for 200$, but if you feel it can help you somehow, I can give you free access and point you to the right videos that will help you. Maybe this way I can help you. I just need your email and I will give you access. Would that be something interesting for you?" Boom! You are still in control of the conversation, you have found a way to provide value, you have offered a gift that solves a specific problem and you got the contact information of your prospect, who is looking forward to reading the next email coming from you.

Let's talk psychology: being in control of the conversation gives you an easy way to communicate what you do and make others feel grateful for your interest and attention. People like to buy from people they like. Offering a gift, triggers the reciprocity principle, one of the most powerful principles in marketing, which states *that the moment you offer something of value for free to a prospect, our shared innate tendency to reciprocate increases the probability of your client making a purchase.* Creating the expectation for a gift arriving in the next email, makes the people look forward to it and open the email. Finally, letting the prospect continuously qualify himself makes him feel that he was the one who decided that your services will be good for him.

Moreover, you achieved something more here. If you created the course correctly, you are offering to your prospect a resource that has been optimized to educate him about your services and market them for you. You have created a reason for you to send him more relevant material that can help his business, such as your blog posts, e-books, checklists, processes, audio files, videos, etc. Also, you have a reason to call him a few days after you gave him access and simply ask if he enjoyed what he learned, and how he is planning to apply it. Now you can ask him if he has any doubts, and you can let him know that if he wants expert advice or support, he knows where to find you. There is no hard selling involved here, but I can guarantee you that if this client ever decides that he needs services like yours, you will be the one he will call.

Now, everything that I described in the previous paragraphs except the phone call by you, can be automated. A simple email sequence can follow up, giving access to all the other resources. If this email sequence can be connected to your course management platform, then it can deliver content at the right time (like right after your prospect has finished watching a video or the course). This kind of timing is powerful and increases conversions. The only thing you need to do is to give access to the course, and most of the follow-up process is done automatically. This is your marketing funnel, the process that makes sure your prospects remember of you more often and for the right reasons.

That was one more way to use an online course to get clients. Obviously, there are plenty of ways to optimize both the course and the follow-up process, and the better you understand marketing, the higher the conversions.

If you decide to ask for help, feel free to reach out. We can help you bring fellow professionals that you would like to create a team with, hook you up with the new teams that are being built and provide the resources you need to explain to other professionals how to easily create the courses they want. Together, we can help you find more ways to save money, frustration and time, while creating a marketing system that will pay for itself many times over, as we saw in the previous chapters. We'll take care of all the technical part, the course editing and hosting, email automation, customer support related to any technical issues. We can help you understand what content needs to be in the course and how to communicate it. We'll show you what tools to use to record the course, and how to record a great course, even if you can't remember a single line of what you want to say to the audience.

But if you feel that the money you are saving by not asking for professional support, the lower conversions and the extra time that you will need to invest in creating the course alone are worth the trouble, then keep reading the next chapters which will guide you through the process, touching the following topics:

- What to teach in your course
- How to structure your course to increase its marketing capabilities
- What equipment you need to record a professional looking course
- How to record your course even if you can't memorize anything
- Tools to edit your course
- Where to host your course
- A few additional ways to distribute your course to get additional clients
- How to make sure you increase conversions by setting an automated email process

The intention is to show you the right direction and give you a few tips to make your course creation easier.

To help you on your path, even if you decide to walk it alone, you can still send us an email telling us what you are helping clients do and the course you are thinking to create, and we'll be happy to give you a few more tips and ideas, or even have a quick call and have a real conversation. We also have a monthly draw where we choose one of the ideas and help the professional create the course without any fee.

Time to create your course

n the following chapters, we'll discuss the main elements that you need to be aware of when creating an online course. It is intended to be read by experts and business owners who want to get more clients, generate more profit per client and make existing clients return more often, by using online courses.

As we covered extensively in the book till now, applications of the strategy of the online courses for businesses with existing clients can generate relatively easily from $8000 all the way up to $50000 or more. Of course, this can only be done if you use the online courses in combination with the strategies explained in the book.

Here, we'll focus on the technical and marketing side of creating courses. We'll discuss:

1. How to find what to teach in your course.

2. How to structure your course to increase its marketing capabilities.

3. What equipment you need to record a professional looking course on a low budget.

4. How to record your course even if you can't memorize anything.

5. Tools to edit your course.

6. Where to host your course.

7. A few additional ways to distribute your course to get additional clients.

8. How to keep in mind if you want to increase conversions by setting an automated email process for your course.

How to find what to teach in your course

A t the end of the day, all you need is 10 powerful tips for your viewers. *Most, if not all of those tips, must be immediately implementable and able to give results fast when implemented*. All of those tips *must* be related to a bigger, more valuable service that you are providing as a paid offer. You might already have in your mind 10 tips that your clients find quite valuable. Below, we will go through a process of asking different questions to find more tips and valuable advice, but for now, just write down what comes immediately in mind. Don't worry if you don't have ten or if you are not certain yet which to ideas to could you share; we'll deal with that in a while. Just write what you have in mind.

Got it?

Now, let's go a bit deeper:

In its core, what you need is to create a course that has the potential to take people from where they are to a better place they want to go. *People do not buy features, they buy transitions*. Once they are clear about the transition you are willing to help them make, believe that you can offer that transition, and want that transition, they buy.

Think about it. When you go to the dietician, you don't pay for the diet plan. You pay for the transition from your current weight to your target weight. When you buy a microwave, you don't buy it because of its functions. You buy it because you want to go from waiting 20 minutes for your food to heat in the oven, to merely clicking a button and having it ready in 2 minutes. These are transitions.

53

To figure out which transition you should offer to your client simply ask:

Why most clients come to me in the first place? What are they looking?

From my experience while managing Open Circles Academy with a history of 150000 clients, I found out that most business owners *think* they know the answer. But if you really want to know, I suggest you start asking your existing clients.

Your goal is to get specifics. It would help to ask yourself and your clients the following questions:

- where do they want to go?
- What's the A to Z that they are looking for?
- If you were at the beginning of the journey your clients are in, what advice, tip, insight, shortcut would you love to know to get fast from A to B, or D, or M? Shortcuts are powerful. If a person is willing to buy a transition, that person will be happy to pay double the price to get a shortcut and get that transition to happen easier, faster, simpler.
- "Common mistakes to avoid" go hand in hand with shortcuts. What kind of mistakes most people do? How could they avoid them in the easiest way possible?

Let's add all the ideas that you can generate to the previous list of ideas you had:

- Write down the transition you will offer to your clients.
- Write down the shortcuts you wish you had if you were at their position.
- Write down the common mistakes and how to avoid them.

Tip:

For this kind of processes, I usually create a mind map. If you are not familiar with what a mind map is, simply go to Youtube and search for "How to use Xmind". You can download the app or the software for free on www.xmind.net. Then, you just need to add your ideas inside a Topic. Once you have enough ideas, you can drag and drop, expand, add comments etc. Try it out!

Now that you have already a few ideas, start asking the questions below. This will give you additional ideas related to the context of each idea, and might remind you additional tips you can give. Don't worry if you start having too many ideas. The purpose of this is to create as many as possible, and then select the most fitting ones.

- How, what, when, who, why?
- What could simplify that?
- How can my clients get faster results?

Now that you have enough ideas, start asking yourself:

- Is there a way to put all of it in a process?
- How do people go from A to B, then to C and then to D?
- What makes sense to be heard first, what after?

Rearrange the tips.

Got it? Good.

Now let's try to get some more ideas out there. The following questions come from a simple realization: when a client comes to have a session with you, she wants to get the maximum results possible. For you to describe the online course as a natural addition to your existing services, you may ask the question:

- Can I help her multiply the results she is getting from my sessions?
- What does she need to see, be reminded of, or practice at home to be more successful, to see more results or to be better prepared for the next session with me?

This might give you some extra ideas.

Now I want you to select the ideas that seem more suited to help your clients achieve the transition your course offers.

For each of the ideas that you selected, ask yourself:

- What is the one action you want them to take after each tip? Define it and explain it.
- What can stop them from taking that action? Give them tips to overcome those obstacles.

By now, you should have those ten tips you need for the course, together with the actions your clients need to take after listening each tip, shortcuts, advices to achieve results easier etc. This is your primary content for the course. Now, you need to increase the "marketing capabilities" of your course. In simple terms, you need to make the viewers get hooked and engaged, educate them on the benefits and transitions your services offer without being salesy (we'll discuss the principle of "pre-suasion" soon), and offer your services in an irresistible way. You need to do that while you are delivering your primary content. Now, this is both an art and science, but the following chapter will give you a good solid base.

How to structure your course to increase its marketing capabilities

To make sure that your course is helping you market your services you need to make sure you understand a bit of marketing. *Marketing at the end of the day is nothing more than making people know you, like you, trust you, try your products or services, buy from you, repeat buying and finally talking favorably about you to other potential clients.* The job of your marketing is to systematically move people from knowing you all the way to talking to others about you. As we discussed in the first part of the book, an online course can help your clients do all those things, if set correctly.

Now, we'll break the whole course into three areas which I call "beginning", "during" and "offer". I will share with you a few tips for each.

Beginning

The first thing you need to do is to realize that for a person to watch a full course (even if it is just a one hour video), that person needs to desire something that this course promises. Your first job then, is to remind them of the reasons they have to watch the video. This is where you can "sell" them the transition that you identified in the previous chapter. As we discussed in the first part of the book, there are four main reasons a person buys:

1. To make more money, now or in the future.

2. To save more money, now or in the future.

3. To live a better life, now or in the future.

4. To save time, now or in the future.

Ask yourself, what of all those things I do? If you help people lose weight or improve their health, then you are helping them create a happier life. If you are helping them grow their business, you might be helping them with any of those four. If you feel you are doing something that is not included in those four categories, then feel free to add it.

Your first video's job will be to remind them what they will get if they keep watching. In marketing terms we call that WIIFT: "What's In It For Them?" *You need to include reminders of the reasons they need the transformation this course is offering.*

The second purpose of the first video, which is closely related to the first, is to keep the viewers "locked". What this means is simple: you want to make people curious. *To make someone curious, you need to make him experience a "knowledge gap". A knowledge gap is created whenever a person does not understand how he can get from where he is to where he wants to go.* Let me give you an example.

When people ask me what I do for a living, I don't say that I help clients create online courses and use them to get more clients, and increase their revenue per client. I say: "I help small business owners and experts get more clients and increase their income while sleeping." This is a knowledge gap. If that person is a potential client that can use my services, he will become curious to learn more, and he will ask. Now I know he is curious and and I have his permission to explain more. He is looking for a way to "fill the gap".

A second example I can give is the following. For some specific potential clients, my answer is "I help business owners focus 95% of their time on the thing they love more doing in their business." Let me explain. For a long time, I have been creating referral systems for small business owners. In other words, I help them get more word of mouth for their services systematically. Word of mouth is one of the most powerful ways to get potential clients ready to buy from you.

In some cases, the entire marketing can be exclusively referral based. In Open Circles Academy, more than 90% of the clients for the Business Bootcamp came from referrals; 90% of 22 Milion Euros of revenue, you can do the math. When I meet a potential client, especially from the expert business (such as coaches, consultants, speakers etc), I know that they usually spend more time in trying to get clients than actually helping their clients. I help them create a referral marketing system so that their existing clients will bring them new clients. This way, all they have to do is to focus on providing an excellent service for their clients. The rest happens almost automatically.

You need to create a similar knowledge gap for your clients. A specific technique we use is called "Creating Open Loops". Let me explain how that works with an example. Imagine you are a dietician and you say "During the course you will learn how to lose 5% of fat. You will do that without reducing the calories you eat or even the kind of food you eat." That's an open loop combined with a knowledge gap. Most people have already heard that to lose weight you need to eat less or healthier. When you tell them that there is a hack that can allow them to lose weight, while eating the same quantities and type of food, this creates a knowledge gap. At the same time, you "open a loop"; people learned that there is a way to get their results, but they don't know yet how. They need to watch the course to "close the loop". (By the way, if you are curious, this method to lose weight is called fasting. It helped me lose weight fast and permanently while feeling more energetic and focused. A life-changing book on the health benefits of this method is The Complete Guide to Fasting and you can find more about it in the resources page growyourbusinesswithonlinecourses.com/resources.

The third thing you need to do in the first video is to set the right expectations. Be clear on what exactly they will be able to do/achieve/feel once they watch the complete course. Do not overpromise, just focus on what you actually give. Set the right expectations. At the end of the day, you don't want people to lose their time. If what you are going to offer is not enough for them, then it is better to know it from the beginning.

There is something very specific that you need to add in the video. I call it the "This is what you get from the course. This is what you get from me personally." segment. This is what I say to the people that are taking a course from me on how to use courses to grow their business: "Right now you are watching a course that will provide you the basic knowledge you need to have to create courses that can increase the number of your clients, get more revenue per client and make clients come back more often. This is what this course gives you. And you can do a decent job alone if you follow my advice. Business owners have increased their revenues all the way up to 26% just by implementing what is in the course. If this is enough for you, then you will love this. I created this course based on my work with many clients over the years. It is based on the experience I have while working with each one on identifying what needs to get in the course, editing the script using copywriting techniques that I have learned while communicating with thousands of clients and prospects. It is also based on my experience taking care of the editing and hosting of multiple courses, the digital part of the communication plus customer support related to any technical issues, and exploring the customer journey and the entire marketing process to identify how to multiply the effects of a single course and get it in the hands of as many people as possible. Just in Open Circles Academy, in a single year, more than 1 Million Euros worth of online courses was sold. This is what I help clients do, and this course will give you a solid basic understanding of how you can do that, should you choose to do it alone." This is an application of the "This is what you get from the course. This is what you get from me" principle.

The reason you need this segment is the following: people need to hear what are the services you offer, what are your results, what are your credentials. They need to know what you are capable of giving them. You don't want to do any hard selling; you just want to let them know. I want my viewers to know that if they want to have an expert to help them avoid mistakes and increase the effectiveness of their course, I can help them. I am not pushing for a sale; I am just letting them know. You need to do the same. Let them know based on what knowledge and experience you created this course. This will allow you to tell them what your services are.

So, take a moment now and write down:

1. How are you going to remind them of the reasons they have to watch your course?

2. What loops can you open, so they get curious?

3. What exactly are they going to be able to do/achieve/feel when seeing the course and implementing your advice?

During

L et's move to the "During" part. Here we will deal with what you can do, while teaching your ten tips, to improve your marketing. All the ten videos, are here to prepare the audience and educate each viewer so that by the time you give your offer, they will be ready to buy. You need to persuade them -before- you give the offer. This is called in one word "Pre-suasion". A beautiful introductory book on this topic is called "Presuasion" and you can find the link to it in the resources page growyourbusinesswithonlinecourses.com/resources, if you want to explore this alone.

To pre-suade, you need to do four things:

1. Set the frame
2. Seed
3. Raise objections
4. Engage with further proof.

Setting the frame

In every situation you deal with, there is an invisible frame around it that sets the tone. When an employee talks with the boss, the frame might dictate that "the employee's opinion is *an opinion*, but the boss' opinion is the final decision (ouch!)". The boss's frame is stronger than the employee's frame. When you are a world class expert, and you are answering a question from the audience, the frame might be that "what comes out of your mouth is wise and correct." The "expert frame" is stronger than the "audience's frame".

The important thing you need to remember is that the person who controls the frame, controls the situation. The person with the stronger frame gets the most out of any situation. Although there is a full book on controlling the frame called Pitch Anything that you can check on growyourbusinesswithonlinecourses.com/resources, I just want you to focus on a specific example: the process of acquiring a new client.

There are two frames that "collide", and the stronger one wins. On the one side, you have a client, who feels that he is paying you, so he is in control. *You* need to convince *him*. On the other hand, you have the frame of the business owner. You have a valuable service to offer, and the client is in need for that service. Which frame wins? Well, it depends on the skills of the two parties.

Let me give you an example from Open Circles Academy. At one point there was an offer to live for a week at the house of the founder and get 1-on-1 help on how to improve your marketing. The cost for each person was 25 thousand euros. You would assume that each client felt that he had the stronger frame. After all when you pay €25k, you expect to be treated as a prince. Well... That's not how the actual story went. Each person that wanted to join, had to pay a small fee to apply. Then, he had to explain what his business is doing and what is his commitment. Then he had to be interviewed by the partner of the founder, and only if the partner decided that the business owner was ready to do what it takes to grow the business, then he had to pass from an interview with the founder. The clients during the process mentioned many times that "although I am going to pay you €25k, I still feel like if I was in a job interview and I want the position." That's a change of frame. Open Circles Academy's founder communicated that he is only going to accept certain kind of clients and that he doesn't need the money of anyone. He wants to work with the people he loves working with. And as simple as that, he took control of the frame. You want to do the same thing in your course.

You are giving this course from the position of an expert, of a person who knows what she is talking about. You are offering value that the client needs, you are describing a desirable transition. You don't need the client. You are here because you love doing what you do, and you are here to help people that want to be helped. Keep that in mind while creating the script for your course. Make sure that you say something related to what I explained above. Mention a story (if it is true) where you answered "no" to a client that wanted to work with you and rejected his money, just because you saw that the person was not ready to apply your advice. Mention about moments in your business where the clients were coming after you and not the other way around. Mention examples of clients that came as referrals from your existing clients. Build the frame.

Seeding

Getting the sale is like collecting a tomato from your garden. If you have done your job correctly, you have put a seed in the ground, offered enough water and made sure the earth was nutritious, then it should be easy to have a big, round, red tomato in your hands. The same thing with a sale. You need to seed long before you collect.

If you are not familiar with seeding in marketing, it means *putting the seeds for the future sale in peoples minds way – before- you do any effort to close that sale.* When you hear experts on life transformation telling you their personal story of how they were exactly like you and then made one decision, and their whole life changed to something else, something that you desire as well, they are seeding. Most of the times they will not tell you what that decision was right away. They will tell you their previous situation and their current. This way they raise your desire, you want that solution, even though you don't know if you have to pay for it or is it free. And that's important. A lot of people just mentally switch off when they realize they have to buy something, and they stop listening to what you say the moment they feel you are trying to sell something to them, even if it is something they need and that is good for them. But, if you make sure they keep an open mind and continue listening to you for as long as possible before they feel they need to make any purchase decision, your conversion increases. In other words: if you manage to make people desire your solution and decide they need it before you tell them that you are willing to give it to them as a product or service, you will get a lot more clients.

So, looking at your ideas (the ten tips) and the services you are selling, ask yourself:

1. How can I increase the desire for the results that my services bring?

2. What stories can I casually include that showcase how my services helped people?

3. What desirable transitions can I include? (clients that went from A to Z, problems solved, going from an undesirable situation to a desirable one)

Now, when you read the previous sentences, you might not be sure what the right answers are. That's OK. It takes years of practice on seeding to do it correctly. During the Business Bootcamp of Open Circles Academy, more or less one thousand small business owners every time were listening to a single speaker for two days. It took two days of masterful seeding, focusing on one product: the Master Entrepreneur. But becoming an expert in seeding is worth your time, energy or money. In just one Business Bootcamp more than 250 people bought a 3997 Euros product. In case you wonder, yes, that's more than one million Euros of sales in one weekend. One out of 4 people that were in the room bought.

When I am talking with potential clients and offer my services to help them understand how to seed during the courses, I ask them: how much would you be willing to pay to get 100 new clients? Would you be willing to pay 20% of the revenue those clients generate? 30%? If you knew you could invest 10$ in your business and get 50$ out of it, then it is straightforward to decide what to do next. Those questions are part of the seeding process, and they are crucial. If the person is not willing to invest to get more clients, then I am not interested in offering my services. But if the person is willing to invest a certain amount, and I charge less than that, then I just "seeded" a comparison price in the person's mind. When I mention my price later on, the prospect will compare it with the price he had in his head, making a favorable comparison. I will explain in a while the second question I ask, while we discuss the next thing you can do to increase the number of clients you get through your courses: raising objections.

Raising objections

What's the one thing that stops people from buying? Objections. People have objections. For example, they might find your solution too difficult, too time-consuming, too complicated, too expensive. These are objections related to your service. Your potential clients might tell you about their objections or not. But they will always think of them.

What most small business owners do wrong in their marketing is that they try to sell without making sure that they eliminate objections to the best of their ability. Let me give you an example, continuing the discussion I started before on seeding.

Some of my clients initially felt that they couldn't afford me. When I realized that, I simply started asking earlier in the process the following questions:

- Can you afford not getting 10/20/30 more clients per month?

- Can you afford to spend so much money on advertising and then have a client come for only one session with you?
- Can you afford to continue spending money monthly for advertisement?

What this simply did, was helping the clients understand that not investing in a proven method for customer acquisition and retention, is something they really can't afford doing. I made sure to ask those questions early on. By the time I offer to help them, cost is no longer an issue. They can already see the financial benefits of investing in their business.

What about the "too difficult, too time consuming, too complicated" part of the objections? I made sure they knew that if we work together:

- they will have my full support;
- they will know exactly how to select their tips,
- I would personally make sure the course was optimized in terms of marketing,
- I would explain every part of the process of recording the video,
- I would take care of the editing and hosting of the course,
- I would take care of all the digital part related to the email communication with clients and technical support,
- I would even create the content for the emails.

They only need to work with me to identify the tips they want to share and record the videos. For the people who chose for a premium service, I would also work with them to improve the overall process they have to acquire clients, build their referral system and much more.

There is another objection that comes often, but in most cases, unless you are starting now, you shouldn't have that problem. The objection the client has in the back of his mind is: can you actually do all the things that you promised? Now, if you are working for years in this field, you shouldn't have problems with that question, if you have done the right things. If you have projects that you worked on and the results were outstanding, or you worked with prestigious clients or projects way bigger than the project you are offering to work on with your clients, then you need to make sure your potential clients know about it.

For the last part (bigger projects) make sure you stay close to your clients' situation. You want to pass "The Frank Sinatra test", but not alienate your potential clients. What is the "Frank Sinatra test"? Well, you probably have heard the song "New York, New York". Well, in that song, Frank is basically saying: New York, if I can make it here, I can make it everywhere. That's *the Frank Sinatra test: a single example, that shows to people that you did something way bigger than what you promise.*

In Open Circles Academy we did a huge transition from a "local" business to a digital business. What that means, is that courses that were given during events had to be moved entirely online. We are talking about million Euros worth of education content. And then everything had to be managed online. In simple terms that meant building websites, managing email automation and newsletters for 45000 people, hosting and managing online courses, creating email campaigns to up-sell and cross-sell different courses, writing copy that converts/blog posts/sales emails/landing pages, creating lead magnets, writing books, managing technical support. And the founder of Open Circles Academy, a multi-multi-millionaire chose me to work with him. This one project qualifies me as a person that can deliver such services. This is my Frank Sinatra test.

A similar situation applies to my offers to help business owners build a referral marketing system that brings them clients almost automatically. In Open Circles Academy more than 90% of the first time clients came because of its referral system. And this was simpler to achieve than what you could potentially imagine. Then, tens of thousands of clients learned how to improve their referral systems. Being the CEO of Open Circles Academy, creating content and simplifying the way clients could build effective referral systems is one more of my "Frank Sinatra" qualifications.

But, while a project way bigger, and way more complicated than what I offer to clients that I help might be a great way to show expertise, a lot of clients immediately think: "Yes, but these were projects with plenty of funding and many people that helped. I don't have the funds for that or the people." This is where simpler stories come in place. When you have established your positioning and expertise, you need to stay close to your target audience. For example, in the first part of the book, I talked about this one spa for which I developed the concept for both their online courses and their referral marketing. This spa was not a multinational chain, the budget was not infinite, the resources and time were limited, and the business had to continue operating in real time. It was a spa as many others, whose owner had two simple problems:

- although the service was great, a lot of clients that he got through ads didn't come back, and
- current clients, even the ones that were very satisfied, rarely brought a new client.

Both those problems are easy to tackle with the use of online courses.

As you can see, this is a story that relates naturally with small business owners, and most importantly, it helps deal with objections.

Your job is to ask yourself: do you pass the Frank Sinatra test? Do you have a single client or project that builds your credibility? If the CEO of a multinational company comes to you for your services, that means you have been pre-qualified. If a TV presenter is coming to you for their Yoga session, this is a credibility booster. Think of what is the single, most important piece of information your potential clients need to know about your business. Make sure to include that as a story in the beginning of the course. It can be in the introduction, or it can be during the first videos. Make the story relevant to the tips and maybe extract a valuable lesson out of it.

Overall, think of all the potential objections a client might raise when the time to decide if he/she buys, and include stories and examples about it during the course.

Calls to Action

I will only briefly touch this point, but I think it is important to have a notion. To continue educating your audience and building your credibility, you might want to include Calls to Action during the course. This means

- asking them to follow a link to learn more about something you mentioned (could be a blog post that you have already created, a free resource that you are offering),
- telling them to pick up the phone and call you, or
- simply taking a moment to do a self assessment that will show them potential reasons they might not be getting the results they want in their life or business.

In Open Circles Academy, the last option was used consistently. Our audience had to do quick self-assessments focusing on their business and financial results. When people reach themselves to the conclusion that they are spending too much money on advertisement, that their first-time clients don't come back often enough, that their satisfied clients don't bring new clients, etc., then they have already convinced themselves that they need what we offer. They are already sold, and we just need to inform them how to get what we offer. You need to do the same for your clients. It might be a simple, quick 3 minutes assessment, or a checklist, or simply answering honestly three questions.

Overall, ask yourself:

What actions do I want people to take during the course that will increase the number of people that will decide to buy from me? Put some ideas down, and see where you could include them during the course.

The Offer

Till now, we have seen how to identify the content of your course, and how to improve its marketing capabilities. Before we move to the equipment that you will need to use, let's discuss the final part: the offer.

This is the time where all the preparation you did during the course must get converted to results. This is the place where people need to decide. Let's see how.

First of all, remember that in the beginning and during the course you opened some loops. You gave your audience a sneak peek of potential transitions without giving them all the information on how to achieve them. Some of those loops that you created early on, you already closed them by giving them your tips and advises. People were not certain how to get from A to C or D, and you helped them do it. Now they know you have the knowledge and experience to help them achieve the transformation that you promised them at the beginning of the course and they trust you. But some loops should still be open. Usually, these are questions on how to get all the way to Z. This is the time to tell them more about your services and how you can help them get to Z. So, simply tell them that by the end of this video they will know what they can do to get to Z.

Before we see how to do that, I want to remind you that they are already warmed up, since during the course you have already included stories of people getting to Z using your help. They had already a sneak peek, and they probably felt desire for what other people achieved. Your job now is to "stack" all the positive emotions they had during the course. In other words, *your job is to bring everything they want in mind right before they take the decision*. And then, you want to add a bonus to that. This is how to do it:

First, you need to remind them of the transformation they want. Do they want to make more money, save more money, live a better life or save time? Make sure to remind them. Experts in that field are using imagery and visualization together with a mix of emotional hot buttons. This is an advanced technique far beyond the scope of this book, but in simple terms, what you need to do is to create a vivid image in the head of your potential clients of how their life would be after that transformation. Show them how their life would be happier, or how they can be relaxed while their business is growing. Paint the picture and make sure to focus on the final results in their lives. I usually check a list of almost 100 emotional hot buttons and identify which fit best for the potential clients.

As an example: in my field, focusing on the usage of online courses for marketing purposes, I usually stress three points. If you have an optimized-for-marketing online course then:

1. *You have more time*. You see, you can spend more time helping clients instead of looking to get them. You chose to do what you do to help others, and till now you spent most of your time trying to get clients instead of helping them. You might even spent time

to explain your services. Now you can focus on actually helping the clients. How would a day at work feel if the only thing you had to do was to help the people you are passionate helping? Moreover, you probably needed to sacrifice part of your personal time to try to get more clients. We all know that when things become tough in business, the first thing we tend to reduce is the time we spend with our loved ones or doing our favorite activities. Well, now you can have more time to focus on the things that matter to you the most, while your course is doing the marketing for you.

2. *You increase your revenue.* In other words, once you get one client, this client will be reminded of the reasons he needs you and will come back more often. The course will give him additional resources so that he will see more results, so he will be more satisfied. Imagine how your daily life would look like if you were working with clients that come to your session all excited to discuss an idea or tip you shared with them in the course, and how it helped them achieve something they were looking for. Or, imagine receiving phone calls from potential clients that tell you that their friends showed them one of your videos and after they applied your tip, they saw a result they were looking for. And now they want to work with you. Would that be a great way to do business? Imagine an existing client coming to a session and saying: "Hey, I saw in your course that you also help people do XYZ. That's interesting. Can you tell me more?" How great would that be? Now you are being asked about your other services, instead of trying to find a way to let your clients know.

If you feel at all uncomfortable when you have to sell your services, then you just found a way to do it easily: your course. If you chose to sell the course, then you created an additional revenue stream. People are paying you for the course, not your time. Some people might even buy that course while you are sleeping. Isn't it a great feeling to wake up in the morning, and checking your mobile and see that someone gave you money while you were sleeping?

3. *You decrease your marketing expenses.* Think about it. Once the course is in place, it costs you nothing to give access to more people. You just need their email. Once you use the course to increase the revenue per client, you need fewer clients. Consequently, you need to invest less in getting other clients. Once you increase the number of first-time clients that come back for more sessions, you once again can spend less on advertising to get new clients. Instead of giving a brochure or a catalog which cost and most people don't even check it, you give them access to a valuable course. Instead of offering one free session with you, spending your time without being paid, you offer free access to the course, and you can use this time to increase the quality of your services, making them remarkable, and thus, making people talk to others about them. You can invest all that money that you saved to hire an extra employee to help you, or you can simply choose to use them to take a few more days of vacations with your family, friends or simply alone drinking mojitos in a tropical island if that is what you love doing.

I can keep going on, but you get the point. Show them what your services can do for them and connect it with making money, saving money, living a better life or saving time.

The second thing you need to stack on top of that, if possible, is the "investment/savings angle". This works really well in business settings, and you have seen me doing it already. A lot of people have the objection of price. They feel you are too expensive. Most people focus on explaining why investing one dollar can generate two. And this is great. People need to see that their money is an investment. This is the Investment Angle.

Now, what most people forget is the Savings Angle. You see, people get more frustrated when they lose 10$ they had, than when they don't win 10$ they had a chance of winning. People are more afraid to lose something they have, than not gaining this something if they don't have it. To put it simply: *people are more motivated to take action to protect something they have than to get something they could have.* The fear of loss is a greater motivator than the desire of winning. Now, I basically repeated the same sentence four times, but I really want you to get the point.

When a client tells me she can't afford my services to create a course, I simply remind her that she is paying a bigger price if she doesn't; she has to work more hours, spend more money for marketing, charge less for her services, spend more time explaining the services she offers instead of making money providing them and the list goes on. What I have seen after working with more companies I can remember, is that most people don't realize how much it costs them not creating a marketing-optimized course. Once they do, they buy.

Now, don't get me wrong, the investment angle is also important. If you have a way to show them the monetary benefits of investing in your services do it. I did it in the first part of the book. I explained how certain applications of the online courses for marketing purposes can generate 6000-14100$, some others 6000$-12000$, and how combinations of tactics can lead in some cases to 36400-54600 of additional profit. Now, these are calculations that I do together with my potential clients to show them that not investing in my services is "costing" them the loss of additional profit. Creating an online course is an investment. If you can do something similar, I highly recommend doing it.

To give you some ideas:

1. If you are a nutritionist: show them how much money they statistically save from medical expenses by investing in their health.

2. If you are a happiness coach: show them how much more income (statistically) happier people make. If you are not sure where to find those numbers check the book The Happiness Advantage (link in the resources page growyourbusinesswithonlinecourses.com/resources)

3. If you are a spa owner, show them how happier, more relaxed individuals tend to generate more income, perform better in their relationships and have better health.

As you can see it is not difficult to find the financial benefits of most services.

Let's sum up what we discussed till now:

In the last video of the course, you want to remind them of all the important reasons they have to come to you, and show them that investing in you is the logical thing to do.

Now the time has to come to briefly explain your services. Remember, they already have a good idea of what you offer, if you have done a good job in including the right stories during the previous videos. In this sense, you are reminding them of your services.

For most people, this is already enough, and if they know how to reach you, they will. Some people though need an additional reason.

This is where "Offer stacking" comes into play. You see, most people at this stage already see the value in your services, but they don't desire it enough *at the moment*. This is where they need an additional emotional "push". Your job, is to "stack" some more benefits for the people who decide to take action. Let me give an example related to the online courses.

Once I have described to potential clients about all the benefits, have reminded them about their reasons to create those courses, I simply add the information that if they are OK with it, while creating the courses, I will also take a look at their existing marketing systems and will tell them how to improve them. Moreover, I will give them a couple of quick fixes that will help them increase referrals, beyond the use of online courses to do that. So, suddenly, instead of just having professional support to create the courses, they also get a professional to take a good look at their marketing systems, and they learn a few more straightforward ways to get new clients. This increases the value of my proposal.

What are the additional offers that you can "stack" on top of your main offer? Take some time to write some ideas down. The less time and money those additional offers cost you, the better. If you have a second online course, that promotes another service of yours, this would be the perfect time to add it to the offer. It costs you nothing, it provides value, and it does the marketing for you. What more can you ask?

Now, we reached the end of your final video. Remember that in the beginning you told them that by the end of the video they will know what they need to do to get to Z. This kept them engaged to watch the video till the end. You can finish the video by saying: "You invested some time in learning how to achieve X and Y, and I can promise you that if you apply what we discussed so far you will be able to achieve them easier. If you want to achieve Z, you only need to give me a call at <your number> or send an email explaining what you are trying to achieve at <your email>. We'll help you get X and Y."

This is it. Now, to sum up:

At the beginning of the course, you reminded them what they want to achieve. You promised them to give them tools to achieve it, and you explained to them what they will get from the course and from you.

During the course, while providing the tips, you set the frame, you seeded, you raised objections, and you gave them more reasons to engage with your content or contact you.

At the final video, you reminded them of their reasons again, and you painted a picture of their lives once they have achieved what you can help them achieve. Then, you showed them what they lose if they don't want to work with you, and what they win if they do, you reminded them of your main services, and then you added more value by offering some bonuses.

By now you must have a good understanding of what it takes to create an online course and optimize it for marketing purposes. Our next stop, is to understand how to record it. We'll discuss the equipment, and then we'll discuss how to record it even if you struggle remembering what you want to say. Let's do it!

Equipment, Recording, Editing and Hosting

Equipment

Before we start, let me remind you of something:

At the end of the day, the purpose of an online course is to increase people's trust in you and keep you top of mind. When that happens, people will come more often, will buy more, will recommend you to others. If you set a few systems around your course, those results will be multiplied. Keep in mind though that the first thing you need to do is to increase trust.

So, what is the absolute minimum that you need to have concerning equipment to record a course?

Simply put, a mobile with an HD camera (that you probably already have) with a socket for a lavalier microphone. The lavalier should cost around 15-25$ dollars, and you must make sure it has a long cable (a 79" or 2 meters is usually enough). You can follow the links in the resources page for some good candidates (growyourbusinesswithonlinecourses.com/resources). There are other more expensive options, but after seeing best selling videos from Open Circles Academy being recorded with just this simple equipment, I would say that they are not necessary. Most mobiles can record already great quality videos, and the lavalier microphone keeps the background noise to a minimum. When the image and the sound are good, all you need is interesting and relevant information.

Now, there is one more element that can help you create a great video: light. In professional sets teams of lighting experts can spend anywhere from 15 minutes to 8 hours to light a single shot that might last just 6 seconds in the finished film. You don't have to do that. Modern cameras take care of exposure (light and dark) automatically. But sometimes the automation gets it wrong. Most of the times that happens because we did something that told the automation to do the wrong thing. A few common mistakes: if you have a window or another source of light behind the person that is being recorded, the subject will become dark. The camera finds the brightest light and considers it the "normal". Then everything else becomes darker, and we simply can't see the face of the person. The second common mistake: not enough light in the room. The more light you have, the crisper the images will become.

The solution is simple. Make sure you have enough light shining on the person's face. You don't need to buy an expensive light set (unless you choose to do so). You can simply use a lamp. We usually recommend buying a lamp that has a light temperature of 3000K and between 1000-2000lm (lm is short for lumen, and indicates the intensity of the light. The higher the number, the more light you have). You can check the resources page for some ideas. But even if you can't find that lamp, there are two more solutions:

1. Simply position yourself in front of a window, having plenty of sun falling on your face. As long as the light from outside doesn't change much during your recording, because of clouds temporarily passing in front of the sun for example, and there is no noise coming from the street, you should be fine.

2. Use a simple video editing tool that helps you adjust the light. I would highly recommend using Filmora (check the resources page). It allows you to play with the light and contrast in your videos so even if your shot is not great, you can still do amazing things with it. We'll discuss more about editing in a while.

That's all you need to know concerning equipment. Now, let's discuss the recording process itself.

Recording

Most people that record their first course don't have experience in front of a camera, they feel uncomfortable, and they forget what they wanted to say, or how to say it correctly.

The first thing you will need to do is to forget about the course. Put the camera in front of you, and record for a few minutes yourself talking about your life, imagining that you are talking to your 10-year-old grandson. Then watch the video. What do you see? Should you be closer to the camera? Further away? Most of us tend to sit in the middle of the screen, but it usually looks better to be a bit more to the left or right. Try to change a couple of things and see what happens. For example, instead of looking straight to the camera with both your shoulders and face, try a more relaxed pose, where your shoulders are turned a bit towards the side, while your face looks directly to the camera. This gives a more energetic and casual feel. Are your hands visible or not? If you are using many gestures, you would like people to see them. Keep in mind, you can select only a part of the screen during the editing, so you can always create shots where the camera is focusing only on your face later on, but you can never add parts of the scene that were not recorded. What that means is simple: if your camera is good enough (at least 8MP), you can record everything from the waist up, and later on zoom in while editing the original footage if you want.

The second thing we need to deal with is what comes out of your mouth. During the years I have met many business owners that had difficulty communicating in front of a camera. Most of the time it all comes down to remembering what they had to say. The solution is simple. Write down what you are going to say exactly the way you want to say it. The rule of thumb is that a one hour course usually has 6000-7000 words in it. You can measure the words of your text online by googling "how long will it take to read my text". Many pages will appear to help you find out. Since you have ten tips to share, an intro and an outro, you just need 500 words per video. One page is roughly 500 words. If you have significantly more than that per tip, reduce it or, if you prefer, delete one of the tips. If you have considerably less than that, you can ask questions such as how, why, when, who, which are the common objections, which are the common reasons people wouldn't apply that tip, etc. This will give you ideas.

Now, you already have the tips and the stories prepared so it shouldn't be difficult to write the final text. Bonus: once you have everything in writing, you can also self-publish a book with the information that you shared on the course, or get an editor and then publish a full book. In Open Circles Academy this process was used to create best-selling books like the Elements of Success.

Now that you have your text, you just need to google "free online teleprompter". I like using the one from the whitehatcrew. Put your computer screen right behind the camera, and take a few shots. Your goal is to have the screen as much as possible behind the camera (or mobile) so that it looks as if you were looking at the camera, but at the same time, the camera doesn't hide the screen that much that you cannot see it. Try a few different shots till you find the best balance. See the videos and decide if you should speak slower or faster and adjust the speed of the teleprompter.

Finally, if you are open to doing some advanced editing (or outsourcing it to someone else), you can have a second camera/mobile recording from a different angle and switch between the two.

That's it. Now the only thing you need to do is to actually record your videos. There is no magic trick, just start. Record a couple of videos, see how it feels, see how it looks. Adjust and improve if necessary, and don't be too hard on yourself.

Editing

When it comes to editing, you have two options; you can outsource it or you can do it yourself. If you feel like outsourcing it, I would recommend using Fiverr. In this case you can check the resources page for more growyourbusinesswithonlinecourses.com/resources.

You can get a freelancer to do it for you, and if you keep the editing needs to a minimum you can get it done at a reasonable cost, probably around 500-1000 for all the videos.

The other option is to do it yourself. Now, you are no videographer, so we'll keep things simple. Our goal is to create a good looking video, that communicates valuable information and is enjoyable to watch.

Concerning software, I would recommend purchasing Filmora (check the resources page). If you are in no mood to spend money on a video editing software, then Windows Movie Maker or iMovie might be your solution, since they are both free. When it comes to audio editing, you can get Audacity for free.

Before the start of each video, you will need a quick animation, showing your logo, your website and, unless you don't want to give too much away, the name of the video. You can get something like that on Fiverr for 5-10.

Then, the video with your tip should follow. If you used only one camera, the simplest thing you can do is to... do nothing. After all, it is a 4-5 minutes video of you explaining something to your audience. If you are willing to spend a bit more time, then you can play a bit by changing the scenes, either zooming in on your face, or zooming out. Filmora allows you to select parts of the video, so you can make yourself move from the left part of the screen to the right, giving the feeling that there were more cameras on you. If you used two cameras, then you can change from the one camera to the other.

A quick tip: don't just change frames for no reason. Change only when you start explaining a different aspect (think of it as changing a paragraph). Moreover, if you want to try some advanced tricks, change the shot precisely at the moment you blink. It makes the transition seem more natural.

Now, there are a thousand other things you can do, but this is not a videography course. I highly recommend finding someone to do the editing for you, especially if that person is familiar with creating online courses. It is not theoretical physics, but it still needs to be done correctly.

A simple process to follow when editing is the following:

- Upload the videos on Filmora or any other video editing software you use.
- Listen to the sound of the video. If there is too much static background noise, export the videos as audio, and use Audacity to remove the background noise. If you don't know how, go on Youtube and type "remove background noise audacity" and you will find plenty of videos. You might need to transform the audio into a format that Audacity supports (WAV) online. Simply

google "transform audio to wav" and you will find different options.

- Add and synchronize the edited audio.
- Use Filmora to remove the beginning and the end of the videos, add your logo animation in the beginning or end, and edit the colors and lighting if necessary. If you don't know how to do it, just google "How to Edit Video Brightness on Filmora" or any other tool you are using. Warning: not all tools have this option, especially the free ones.

Hosting

So, you made it. You have your course. Where can you host it? Where can people see it? There are different options, and each of them has its benefits.

Udemy is one of the options. One of the benefits is that they have a vast marketplace so people that are not your clients can find you. The process of uploading the course is also quite straightforward and easy. On the negative side, unless you are willing to allow them to keep selling your course for just 10$, they will probably not promote you. Also, there are many restrictions when it comes to how you communicate with the students and what you can or cannot say. Some course creators have been banned just because they promoted their own services more aggressively or because they included links to their business. Skillshare and Teachable are platforms similar to Udemy, and they have similar restrictions. If you want to use any of them, make sure to read their course requirements.

I usually recommend self-hosting, using Kajabi or Thinkific. There, you have a lot more freedom. You can include promotional content, connect the platforms to email automation software, create the discounts you want, etc. On the negative side, they are not free. You need to pay either monthly, or yearly, and you need to connect your own online payment providers. You can find relevant links on the resources page growyourbusinesswithonlinecourses.com/resources.

The selection of the right platform depends on the kind of content you created and on the way you are planning to use the course to promote your services. For this reason, unfortunately, I cannot give you a rule of thumb, except this: if you can afford it and if your primary purpose with the course is to market your services, you better self host your videos.

In the next chapter, we are going to discuss a few more ways to get additional clients and increase conversions using email automation tools, that we did not present in the first part of the book.

Additional tips on distributing the courses and increasing conversions

We already discussed how to use your course for referral marketing, contact marketing, VIP packages, and team courses to get new clients in the first part of the book. Here, I want to give you a few more ideas to make your courses reach more people.

The first is to create partnerships. The idea is simple: *clients buy easier when they receive more value*. If you have partners that can offer your course as a bonus for what they sell, then they will increase the number of their clients (since the clients receive more value) and you will have more people becoming familiar with your work. You can allow your partners to charge for the course to increase the benefits of the partnership. This option usually works best when the additional cost for the course is quite small as compared to the service your partner offers, and if the target audience of your partner is quite similar to yours. The only thing you need to ask yourself is: who are the professionals that serve similar clients to mine and how can I best describe the value of this partnership.

The second idea that has worked really well, is to create social media sharing incentives for your clients. The idea is to use tools like Upviral, which you can find on the resources page, or similar, and offer free access to your course to people that shared about you on social media. This way, you get access to their network, and you just have to give access to the course to a few clients. For the rest, you can offer other incentives, like a 90% discount for the course for example. You can stretch this idea toward many directions. The main concept is that you can incentivize people to do things for you, using the access to the course as an incentive.

In Open Circles Academy, hundreds of clients each time were sharing posts about the Business Bootcamp all over their social media, to get free access to a 3997$/person course. This generated huge publicity, creating more clients for the next event.

The third idea is the following: you already wrote 500 words for each tip. Why not publish each tip as a blog post? In each blog post add a link to the course. Start sharing the blog posts on social media (organically or through ads). If you are often going to networking events, every time you talk with a person that might be helped by one of the ideas in the blog post, simply ask them for their email and send them the blog post.

A fourth idea would be to send an email to all your ex-clients, thank them for trusting you and give them access to the course. Worst case scenario, they won't do anything. Best case scenario, they will remember why they came to you in the first place and will decide to come back again. Nothing to lose there.

There are hundreds of ways to use a course. The reason is simple: it costs you nothing to give access to it, and it provides value to others. People will be grateful to get access to information that can improve their lives.

Now, let's discuss a bit about email automation. The only reason I am mentioning it is that most people don't understand its power. Emails, if done correctly, can keep you top of your clients' mind, and can give you a way to contact people that used to be your clients but they are not anymore. It costs you nothing to send an email and, as long as the content of the email is valuable, your clients or prospects will be grateful for it.

The way we use it when it comes to courses is the following:

Once a new user has joined a course, we add his email to an automation process, so he receives one email per day, mentioning one of the videos of the course. This will remind them daily of the benefits of watching the videos. Many people start online courses and never finish them, so it always helps to stay in touch. In each email, we also add some extra tips or access to valuable resources. As we approach the last emails, we also add discounts and promotions.

Your goals for each email should be:

- Make them see value in opening your emails. You do that by sending them information and access to valuable content.
- Remind them of their reasons for coming to you in the first place. You can do that by either using the narrative of the email or by directing them to content that reminds them.
- Make them used to the emails. You can do that by being consistent on when you send the emails. Email automation software like Active Campaign can help you do that. You can check it in the resources page.
- Drive them back to your course. Each of the first ten emails can focus on the benefits of watching and applying each one of the tips. You can remind them of the course and send them back to watch a specific video each time.
- Ask them to take specific actions, like contacting you or reading something. In the emails you can give them special reasons to contact you that day or that week. If you have done the previous steps correctly, people will open your emails and will read them. They will feel

grateful for all the additional value you add to their lives, and they will trust you more. More importantly, they will remember the reasons they need your services in their lives.

If you are a bit familiar with email automation, I would highly recommend keeping those five elements in mind. If not, consider hiring someone that does. This is an investment in your business.

Sum up and a suggestion

We just finished a crash "course" in creating a marketing-optimized online course. First, we saw how to find what to teach in your course. Then, we discussed the structure: what needs to be at the beginning of the course and what you should include during the course. Afterward, we examined the part of the offer. Then, you saw that even if you have a low budget, you can afford to buy the equipment that you need. We simplified how you can record your videos through a teleprompter, and we discussed your options when it comes to editing and hosting your course. Finally, we saw some additional tips on how to distribute your course to prospects and clients.

All that might sound like a lot, but at the end of the day, what you really need to do by yourself is decide what you want to talk about in the videos and record them in front of a camera. Everything else can be outsourced.

Having your own online course can revolutionize the way you market your business. Once you have one online course you can attract easier new clients, make your services more desirable, make your existing clients come back more often, allow your clients to talk easier about you to prospects, increase your revenue and so much more. My professional opinion is that anything you invest in making this course better and marketing-optimized is going to help you multiply your results. I am here to help you, based on my experience of helping multiple companies understand the benefits of online courses, creating and selling courses to thousands of clients, communicating by email weekly to as many as 45000 people, managing the online courses of multi-million dollar accounts, and working hand in hand with small business owners that want a more effective way of marketing their services.

If you believe that you can't afford professional help, I invite you to send me your ideas related to the course you would like to create either way, and I or my team will give you a few tips on how to improve it. We run a monthly competition where one applicant per month gets our help without any fees, and we select that person based on the course he/she is thinking to create.

Thank you for taking this time to figure out how to grow your business using online courses. The world needs your knowledge.

Make it a great day,

Dimitris

To find out more about Growing your Business with Online Courses, visit growyourbusinesswithonlinecourses.com

You can find the book's resources at growyourbusinesswithonlinecourses.com/resources

Dimitris can be contacted also by LinkedIn or Facebook.